Home-Based Catalog Marketing

Other Home-Based Success Guides Published by McGraw-Hill

Home-Based Mail Order: A Success Guide for Entrepreneurs
   by William J. Bond
Home-Based Newsletter Publishing: A Success Guide for Entrepreneurs
   by William J. Bond

Home-Based Catalog Marketing

A Success Guide for Entrepreneurs

William J. Bond

McGraw-Hill, Inc.
New York   San Francisco   Washington, D.C.   Auckland   Bogotá
Caracas   Lisbon   London   Madrid   Mexico City   Milan
Montreal   New Delhi   San Juan   Singapore
Sydney   Tokyo   Toronto

Library of Congress Cataloging-in-Publication Data

Bond, William J.
    Home-based catalog marketing : a success guide for entrepreneurs /
William J. Bond.
        p.   cm.
    Includes index.
    ISBN 0-07-006595-0   —   ISBN 0-07-006596-9 (pbk.)
    1. Mail-order business.   2. Home-based businesses.   3. Direct
marketing.   I. Title.
    HF5466.B678   1994
    658.8'4—dc20
                                                          93-36437
                                                              CIP

1 2 3 4 5 6 7 8 9 0   DOH/DOH   9 9 8 7 6 5 4 3

ISBN 0-07-006595-0 (CL)
ISBN 0-07-006596-9 (PBK)

*The sponsoring editor for this book was David Conti, the editing supervisor was
Kimberly A. Goff, and the production supervisor was Donald F. Schmidt. This
book was set in Garamond Light. It was composed by McGraw-Hill's
Professional Book Group composition unit.*

Printed and bound by R. R. Donnelley & Sons Company.

This book is printed on recycled, acid-free paper containing a
minimum of 50% recycled de-inked fiber.

This publication is designed to provide accurate and authoritative information
in regard to the subject matter covered. It is sold with the understanding that
the publisher is not engaged in rendering legal, accounting or other professional service. If legal advice or other expert assistance is required, the services of a competent professional person should be sought.
                    *—From a declaration of principles jointly adopted by a committee
                        of the American Bar Association and a committee of publishers*

To my wife, Janet, who offered love and support for my writing and my life.

Contents

Preface

Yes!

Yes, I know you have thought about starting your own catalog marketing business, but for one reason or another, put it off. This book will be your seminar on how you can utilize your skills, talents, abilities, and interests to produce a catalog which you will be proud to mail out to friends, associates, customers, and future customers.

This book is about helping you make money. There is *big* money in catalogs when you have successfully matched your products to your target market and developed strategies to keep your customers buying from January to December. This book is different because it takes you from ground zero, from selecting the best possible product right through to preparing, printing, and mailing your catalog. No prior experience is needed, only the eagerness to learn the basics and the willingness to keep trying until you get your catalog marketing business working successfully.

It is based on my experience in starting a home-based business, reading, talking to others, and investing in my own career to help you succeed in yours. It is also the result of teaching marketing, advertising, and accounting for 25 years and running my own seminars on catalog marketing.

Focusing on the basics

You can build a strong foundation for your successful catalog by learning all the basics and putting them together for a well-designed and carefully targeted catalog marketing program. This book will help you select the best possible product, write copy, design the catalog, and print and mail it to your best possible target market. You will discover how to see your products and services successfully marketed and keep your customers buying. You will learn how to test the essential elements in your business, such as products, lists, advertisements, prices, offers, and copy approaches. This book shows you how to use many promotion techniques and twenty-first-century public relations strategies and how to manage your business to keep earning money.

Operating your business at home

The real benefit of your catalog marketing business is there is no store to rent, no lease to sign, no office to furnish, no employees to hire; you can start and operate right out of your own home or office. This book shows you how to save time, money, and problems by having the best of both worlds: your own business, operated right at home. Now let's get busy, and go to work—the world of catalog marketing awaits you. We will travel this world together. I promise to inspire and challenge you to succeed.

William J. Bond

1

You can be successful in this business

The catalog business is an exciting, popular, and profitable business. According to the Direct Marketing Association, 13.6 billion catalogs were mailed in 1990, and 100 million consumers purchased by phone. You can present your products and services directly to a clearly defined group of consumers. The opportunities are limitless. There is no expensive lease to sign for 15 years, your location is not necessary in this business; a clearly defined idea is necessary, as is your willingness to keep selling until you succeed. Now let's get started on learning the steps necessary to succeed in this business.

What will make you successful as a catalog business owner?

You will succeed by being creative. By putting together a catalog in an exciting and entertaining style which will help add to your readership. You have the opportunity to present your products and services in the best possible manner, and when you do this you will succeed in this business. I worked with a creative director of a large advertising agency in Boston, and one of his favorite expressions was: "Every product or service has a place in the sun." Just like sun bathers move around into different directions to catch the maximum sun rays, your role in your catalog business is to get the maximum sun or exposure for your products or services. The job of this book will be to give information, techniques, ideas, and insights so you can put together your own winning plan to start your own successful catalog business. We will work together discussing the various products or services and help you choose the best ones and then help you match your products to a specific market or group of people most likely to buy your goods. Once the task is completed the next step will be to develop a marketing plan to sell your products. Nothing happens in your business until a sale is made; this book will help you learn to sell to today's difficult-to-satisfy consumers. Finally, successful catalog owners know success means making a profit in order to stay in the business. A profit is the difference between revenue or your sales and the expenses of running your business. Profit is the engine of your business. For example, let's say you started your business in January, and at the end of the month your accounting records looked like the following:

Sales		$10,000.00
Expenses		
Printing	3,000.00	
Postage	4,000.00	
Advertising	2,000.00	
Total expenses		9,000.00
Profit		$ 1,000.00

Your profits will be your vehicle to help you succeed in this exciting business. Your success will be sustained by your enthusiasm for your idea, your product, service. Nothing is more important than selling a product you believe in and a willingness to give customers complete satisfaction or their money back. This is best summed up in this country's founder of the catalog business for sporting goods, L. L. Bean. The following is included on page 3 of one of their catalogs:

Leon L. Bean founded our company in 1912, offering his new Main Hunting Shoe to a list of Maine hunting license holders. He guaranteed his shoes "to give satisfaction in every way." The rubber bottoms separated from the leather tops on 90 of the first 100 pairs. "L. L." kept his word and refunded the purchase price even tho' it nearly put him out of business. He then perfected his shoes and went on to establish our company based on quality outdoors products backed by an unconditional guarantee. In later years "L. L." wrote: "No doubt a chief reason for the success of this business is the fact that I tried on the trail practically every article I handle. If I tell you a knife is good for cleaning trout, it is because I found it so. If I tell you a wading boot is worth having, very likely you might have seen me testing it out at Merrymeeting Bay."

Your success in the catalog business will come from your belief in yourself, your goods or services, and the unconditional guarantee of everything you sell. Just as L. L. Bean made his company succeed, starting it in the difficult year of 1912, you can make it when you get involved with your business. By trying each product yourself and acting as a customer yourself, you give your customers the best service possible, no matter what costs are involved in time or money. Success means developing your idea, giving quality goods and services.

What is a catalog?

A *catalog* is a book, a leaflet, a file, containing names, articles, and listings. A catalog can be as small as 4 or 8 pages or as large as 99 pages. Most catalogs have pictures, drawings, and photographs of the products and descriptive words (called "copy") next to them in order to motivate the readers to buy from you. Some catalogs only have words and no photographs or pictures. The catalog's role is to entertain the reader, to have the positioned products on the page in a specific manner and written about in such a manner that the reader will act, and buy, from you.

A catalog is not just another selling piece. Too often catalog owners decide to increase their sales by simply putting together some of their products into an unplanned, unprofessional catalog. The result will be disappointing. To get the maximum results, you need to read a book like this one and then put together a catalog which not only sends a message but connects to your preselected market or niche to build a successful and profitable business.

What opportunities are available in a catalog marketing business? A catalog marketing business is your opportunity to present and sell your products or services to people all over the country and the world. Your success is limitless. The only limit or restriction is placed there by you. I like the quote from the philosopher

Santayana in one of his essays: "Knowledge of what is possible is the beginning of happiness." Your catalog business will be a journey, and it can be anywhere you want to go. You determine your success, and this book will help you reach it.

What is marketing?

Marketing is the set of activities directing the product or service from the producer to the customer or user. Marketing is the bridge from you, the catalog seller, to the customer. Marketing success requires your total knowledge of the product or service; total knowledge means you know how the product works, how it is made, and how it can benefit your customers or potential customers. For example, one catalog owner tells readers on the second page of her catalog that she and her staff search the world to bring the best ideas to their readers and enhance their lifestyle and health, and even to help their environment. A good marketing program means trying to change a reader into a buyer and then a loyal lifetime customer to your business. The satisfied customer becomes the fuel of the engine of your business. Successful customers build your business for you.

Marketing means hitting the bull's-eye of your target market. It means when you sell gift items, you try to reach people who buy gift items. Hitting the bull's-eye directly is how L. L. Bean found his market for his newly developed hunting boot—he went to Augusta, the capital of Maine, and copied the names of hunters who recently purchased hunting licenses so he could send them the information on his product. This is clearly one of the most important principles of marketing, to hit the bull's-eye of your target market. Catalog marketing permits you to do so.

Marketing means two things to a catalog marketing business owner: promotion and distribution. Promotion is letting people know that your products are available by your company. Distribution is getting your products into the hands of the people most likely to buy from you. There is marketing in everything you do in your catalog selling business, from choosing the products, to writing copy which will sell them, to pricing, and to mailing your catalogs. Marketing means making your product look as good as possible so your potential customers can understand the total benefits to them and then persuading the prospects to purchase your product. Successful catalog marketers sell products and services that their target market needs.

Marketing is taking your customer or potential customer from the mental stage of just thinking about your product or service, to the physical or action stage, when the customer takes out the pen and sends you a check for one or a number of your products. This stage from the mental to the physical action is one of the most important principles of the catalog selling business. You must create attention and make an impression in your readers' minds that your products or services are special and will add to their lifestyle, can help them make more money, look more attractive, lose more weight; show an openness to your reader that separates you from the rest of the field. In essence you want your reader to vote for you, and the vote is an order for your product.

Marketing means planning your plan and then working your plan. Successful people in the catalog selling business share a common denominator: They are open to new ideas and then have the confidence in these ideas to keep working them until they are successful. Smart marketing will help you stay ahead of the competition. Marketing means looking at new ways to present your product to your customer. Your goal will be to review how your competition markets their product for success. Catalog selling is no different from any other business, it takes hard work, planning, and the ability to keep learning to offer customers the best products and services possible. Marketing takes time and careful planning, and this book will give you all the information you need to develop the best plan possible and then to gather the resources to make the plan work.

What is direct marketing?

Direct marketing is important to you in the catalog selling field because it is any type of marketing which asks for a response from the prospect. You included a coupon, and telephone number, a FAX number, an order form. Your goal will be to get the prospect to respond to you. Direct marketing requires selling on your part. Prospects will become your customers when you sell them on the reasons that it's important to buy from you.

Successful direct marketers know the hot selling points to get the sale, they present the product or service in the most appealing manner possible, offering a gift, perhaps, and taking the time to involve the reader. Getting the reader involved in the catalog will add to the interest and desire to buy your products and services. You will succeed when you focus on acting right now; one catalog marketer states in his catalog "act by November 15th and receive a 10% discount on our products."

What is a market?

A market is a group of potential people with the desire and the purchasing power to buy your product or service. A potential market might be college students, VCR owners, or inspirational book buyers. In order to reach the market you must learn as much as possible about it. How many people are in your market? Where are they located? In the United States? In the world? What makes this market special? What chief characteristics makes it a special market? How is this market changing in the late 1990s and into the next decade? First learn about the market so you can discuss it in great detail, but get to know what the market needs and wants to survive in the 1990s and beyond. How will your products play an important role in your market's life? The answer to this question will be called your special strategies or the bridge which will connect the product to the customer; this bridge will be discussed in a later chapter and is essential to success in your catalog business.

What is a target market?

I remember an adult learner in my college marketing class who raised her hand on the second night of class to ask, "What is the difference between a market and a target market?" My answer then and now is the same: the size of the target.

Instead of trying to sell your catalog product to all college students, you might want to sell to seniors taking business administration at private coeducational universities only, now reducing your target market from 28 million down to 4 to 6 million; doing so gives you an opportunity to focus directly on them.

Successful direct marketers also select the most attractive merchandise possible, keeping the prices in line with the goods, and give clear and simple instructions to order from them. The successful marketers find niches and continue to learn from their victories and setbacks to succeed even more. Everything can be measured in this business. Testing is essential for success. The role of this book will be to make you an aware and successful direct marketer. Take for example a young woman in Massachusetts who recently started her own fresh seafood catalog business by featuring fresh lobster, clambake dinners, and other meals by mail. The dinners are the lead products, which gives this catalog owner a chance to sell butter warmers, plates, pots, audiocassettes featuring sounds of the ocean, and other related items attractive to people who buy her products.

Organize yourself and your catalog business for success. One successful owner of a book catalog business said, "The best way to measure a man's success is his ability to organize his marketing program." This book will help you do this organization for you so your marketing program is a successful process.

What is a lead product?

A lead product is an attractive product sold with a strategy to permit the customer to buy additional products. Once the customers buy from you the first time, your catalog can be sent along in the shipping box, so the customer can buy additional products. Some catalog owners run advertisements in magazines such as *Gourmet, Sports Illustrated,* or *Popular Mechanics* to reach specific groups, and once purchasers buy the lead product, the heavy artillery, your hard-hitting catalog will work to sell more products or services to the satisfied customers. Satisfied customers will keep you in business and help you expand your list of customers, so you can keep mailing new offers to them. Sales result when you find ready and willing customers to buy your product; they are called your "market."

How do you decide on a product or service?

Choose a product which cannot be found in stores. Choose a product or service with which you feel a sense of comfort; choose something you understand and enjoy speaking about and selling without hesitation. Believe in your product; without this belief you will have difficulty convincing others to buy from you. People who believe in their product can communicate more effectively to today's difficult-to-please consumer.

The focus on the product or service is important but not as important as the understanding of why people buy and what people expect from you and your business. Your product or service must be a quality product, but the way you market must also be quality- and benefit-oriented. A nationally known furniture marketer once claimed, "Marketing knowledge is in a very short supply in America, in almost every industry." This book will focus on the selection of the best product for you and show you many different ways to market it as well.

Just to prime the pump, below you will find some sample products and services for your catalog selling business. Remember this list is just a basic list to get you thinking about possibilities; in a later chapter you will be able to complete the process. Mark any product or service with a checkmark which is of interest to you. You will use this information at a later time.

Sample Products

___ Gifts	___ Fishing flies
___ Furniture	___ Clothing
___ Sporting goods	___ Business supplies
___ Books and manuals	___ Pet supplies
___ Tools	___ Wood stoves
___ VCRs	___ Gourmet foods
___ Puzzles	___ Calendars
___ Collection services	

You become an entrepreneur

The entrepreneur is someone who develops an idea for a product or service or a series of products to present and sell to others by use of a catalog and is willing to put up the money and effort needed to succeed. The entrepreneur starts and manages the business. When I discuss the term *entrepreneur* in my seminars on small business and home-based businesses, some students have trouble seeing themselves as entrepreneurs or business owners. The entrepreneur can be a retiree, stock broker, housewife, house-husband, teacher, truck driver, engineer, clerk, computer programmer, and so on. The entrepreneur is a unique person because he or she is willing to take a risk rather than work for a safe paycheck each week. The entrepreneur takes risks, but only after he or she takes a careful evaluation of the catalog marketing business. Be willing to be an entrepreneur. You can do it—just try.

There are numerous advantages to being an entrepreneur: You will have freedom to set up the business of your dreams; you get to carve out the products and services which you feel will sell successfully to your customers. Another advantage is avoiding the politics you had to endure as an employee; no need to get on the right side of your boss, because you now become the boss in your business. You make the decisions, pay the bills, and, when things go well, you get to take in the money.

There are drawbacks as well; you don't get a paycheck like when you work as an employee, you work to make a profit, which means your revenue must exceed your expenses. You will work 60 to 80 hours per week. No one will tell you what to do in your own business. You are in charge of developing your own goals, and you must work hard to reach them. When you set rigid yet realistic goals and then follow through to reach them, you will be successful. You can do it. This book will show you how.

Why are entrepreneurs different from other people?

This is an excellent question. Today's entrepreneurs like the action of doing something which can be meaningful; they can build a business, and when things go well they might even become millionaires. Take the example, of a 32-year-old entre-preneur from California, Kathleen Mahoney, who started her own bridal products catalog right out of her own home, and within one year built sales to over $885,000. Kathleen started the busi-ness because she knew a great deal about brides and bridal products, because she researched the needs of the bride of the 1990s to the fullest. Before Kathleen got married, she shopped for guest books, wedding gifts, stationery, invitations; she wanted to be sure she got the best possible products, since a wedding is a special occasion. Once her wedding was over she knew her interest, background, and researching skills would be very impor-tant in her bridal products catalog marketing business. Kathleen is an entrepreneur because she was willing to take advantage of this special opportunity to use her skills, interests, and knowl-edge to make her business a success.

Just like Kathleen used her skills to start a catalog business, I want this book to be a springboard for you to evaluate your own skills, talents, and abilities and choose the products or services to build your own business. The subject of your business might be the result of your hobby, something you experienced in your life, or from your own job or profession. Open yourself and your imag-ination to select the best catalog subject for you. This book will give you many opportunities to select the best subject for you.

This business is the best of two worlds. You can start a business of your own, become your own boss, and never leave your own home. You have the opportunity to start the business right in the confines of your den, family room, spare bedroom, downstairs office, or even on your kitchen table. The most important part of your business is getting into the cycle of focusing in on your business needs right in your home and of helping your customer.

Successful catalogs know how to keep customers buying. Your success will be the result of your ability to attract customers by having an exciting catalog and keeping the customers buying over and over. Your goal will be to make the customers your customers for life. For example, one catalog owner from Massachusetts, the author of this book, sells books, manuals, and reports on business techniques and time management ideas, and many of his customers have been buying for 15 to 20 years. He started the business on his kitchen table, and now has a 30,000-customer mailing list and a 20-page catalog which he sends out twice a year.

Today's customers are tough, difficult to sell to, and even more difficult to sell to over and over, but when you get everything right, and customers have confidence in you and your offerings, they will buy over and over. Success is when they keep buying.

Summary

This $14 billion-a-year business is an exciting opportunity for you. Your success will result from being creative, selecting the best product or service, and earning a profit. A catalog can be as small as 4 pages or as large as 99 pages. Your catalog marketing business offers you an opportunity to present and sell your products or services. Knowledge of marketing and direct marketing is essential to keep your business growing. You must select a target market and develop strategies to reach it. Good marketing means setting a plan and putting it to work. You decide on a product or service you believe in fully—a good lead product starts the success process. You become an entrepreneur, with all the advantages and drawbacks to it. Let's now discuss organizing your home office.

2

Organizing
your home office

Many businesses are being started right on the kitchen table and can grow to multimillion-dollar businesses. A New York–based market research firm, Link Resources, found that over 39 million Americans do all or part of their work at home, a 56.6 percent increase over the last 5 years. For example, many catalog and mail order businesses started right at home, many sales representatives carry on business activities at home, and service-oriented businesses such as consulting, publishing, and catalog marketing can be based right at home. For example Lillian Vernon Mail Order, Ben and Jerry's Ice Cream, Estee Lauder Cosmetics, Walt Disney Productions, Reader's Digest, and Hallmark Greeting Cards all started right at home. You can do the same.

Set up your office

Choose a spare room

Start your home-based business by setting up your office in a room or space in the basement, family room, or attic. Choose a location away from the television, VCR, or other noisy sections of your home. Once you choose a room or space, go there every day if possible, spend time there getting started with your catalog ideas. Getting into a habit of going to your office will build discipline into your routine.

Start with a good desk

The focal point of your office can be your desk. If your budget does not allow for a desk, you can use a large table; one business owner from Massachusetts started with a large kitchen table for his desk. Choose a desk which will be large enough for your needs.

Get a chair with support for your back

You will be sitting for many hours at your desk, so try to choose a chair which both is comfortable and supports your back. Many used office furniture companies sell excellent used chairs for less than half of the new price. Some business owners prefer a chair with rollers on it for easy movement around the office. You might be able to get both a used desk and chair together at a used furniture store; as your business grows, additional desks can be purchased.

A file cabinet keeps you organized

In the catalog marketing business the most important activity will be testing lists, products, themes, prices, and ideas, and you will need a good system to keep the proper control on your decisions. Your file cabinet can hold essential accounting records you need for your tax preparation as well as your reports, including cancelled checks, deposit slips, bank statements, sales slips, invoices from suppliers, receipts for items purchased for cash, and other related documents or records to help you manage and control your business. A system of filing which permits access to information is essential to your success.

Your telephone is essential

Many of your customers will place their orders to you by phone. Once you get your first catalog in the mail it will be essential that you have a telephone so you can handle the orders, questions, and communications from your customers. Many customers would rather call than fill out even a simple order form. Many catalog houses are finding a larger and larger percentage of their orders placed by phone than by mail-in orders. Some catalog owners use 800 numbers. One catalog marketing business owner from Minnesota has his telephone hooked up to an answering machine which takes messages when he is out of the office. This answering machine is very important when you are working dur-

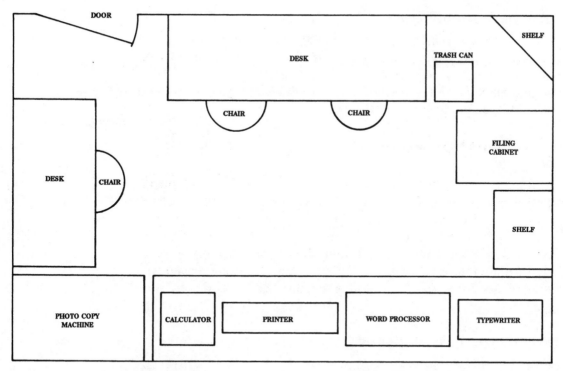

Figure 2-1. Home office layout. This office layout will give you many ideas about how to turn your spare room, attic, or basement into a comfortable and efficient home-based office area.

ing the day or away from your home office. Every call is important to your success.

Keep your office light and cheery

Many home-based business owners set up their office without looking at the color of their surroundings. A den or basement office with a light color or off white or light grey will improve the appearance. It might be as simple as buying a gallon of paint with a painting roller and brush and paint it yourself to make your surroundings substantially better.

Lighting Counts

Good lighting can make your office feel secure and look more spacious. One home-based business owner in New Jersey uses shaded lamps with 3-way bulbs because he prefers indirect, subtle lighting. Other home-based business owners prefer fluorescent lighting. Try various alternatives until you get the best lighting program to meet your needs.

Get your own bookcase

Use a large open bookcase to hold the books, directories, and magazines which you use on a regular basis. One home-based catalog marketing owner from Pennsylvania keeps a file of competing catalogs on the bookcase and reviews it regularly to keep up with the changes in the business.

Move to the best location possible

A home-based business owner in Kansas set up her office in her basement, but being located near the washing machine and dryer made it hard to concentrate and focus on the needs of her business. She solved the problem by moving upstairs to a little-used den and now works full-time running her catalog marketing business selling lamps all over the country. Another home-based catalog owner in a studio apartment used a room divider to save space.

Use the space regularly for your business

In order to deduct costs for your home-based business you must use it each day or regularly, and the space must be used exclusively for the sole purpose of your business. For example, you cannot write off a portion of your kitchen area, when for four to five hours a day it is used for preparing meals for the family. The Internal Revenue Service may review the portion of your home during an audit to determine business use in order to receive the deduction on your taxes. If your home or apartment is 1200 square feet, and your home office takes up 120 square feet, you can deduct 10 percent of all expenses generated by the entire home or apartment including electricity, water, heating, and others. Keep good records on these deductions, just in case you need to produce them at a later date.

Watch your insurance and legal coverage

In order to protect yourself and your assets, it's a good idea to sit down with your insurance agent and discuss your intention to start a catalog marketing business based out of your home, so you can put the best insurance program together to protect yourself, your assets, and your loved ones. Some home-based owners are concerned about having the liability insurance to protect against users or buyers of their catalog products. When you review your insurance, check with your attorney to determine which is the best business organization for you. Your attorney will help you review some important considerations you might overlook in the pursuit of starting your business.

What business organization do you use?

You can choose a number of different organizations to start your business. One is the sole proprietorship, in which you supply the money necessary to get started and you get all the income and the losses which result from this business. Many home-based business owners like the fact that they can get started quickly, avoiding the excessive paperwork of the partnership or corporation, but remember that you will be personally liable for the business losses and other business liabilities.

Other catalog owners prefer to set up a partnership. In a partnership form of organization, you decide to make an agreement with another business associate to start the business together, sharing the responsibilities and money requirements. For example, one catalog business in New Hampshire is run by two owners, one does all the purchasing of products, the other partner handles the day-to-day operations. The partnership organization is based on an agreement by two or more people, and in writing must be the names of partners, duties of partners, and money invested, and must show how profits and losses are distributed. This document must be drawn up by an attorney and signed by all partners in the business.

Other home-based business owners choose the most formal business organization, the corporation. In a number of cases the corporation can limit your personal liability. Corporations are more heavily regulated than other organizations, and to set up the corporation you need a charter from your state, a board of directors, officers, and shares of stock. Filing requirements and specific conditions vary from state to state. Check with your attorney to select the best organization for you.

Research licensing requirements for your business

Call or write to your town or city clerk's office to determine the license or permits required to start your catalog business. Remember to state the fact that you will primarily be mailing information and shipping orders, and you will not be selling from your home. You will not be operating a business which sells on a retail basis from your home. The retail operation would take a much different license than simply a catalog or mail order business. Once you determine what license is required, follow through with the necessary paperwork and payments to complete the process. It is much easier to start your business once the required license or permits are completed. You can then get involved with selecting your product and producing and mailing your catalog.

Manage your time

When you have your office at home, it becomes very easy to watch the extra 5 or 10 minutes of the news or talk program on television, to talk longer to friends, associates, or neighbors on the phone. Don't fall into that trap. Set some daily goals for yourself. What do you want to accomplish today? Start the most important job early in the day, and continue until you complete it. Save errands, making copies, sending faxes, and telephone calls for later in the day when you can group these jobs together. In the catalog marketing business you must focus on today but have the ability to plan 6 months to 1 year ahead. Visualize your catalogs in the mail in 6 months. Those full performance days, filled with high priority items, will help you reach your long-term goals. Goal-oriented people succeed in this exciting business.

Consider these accounting issues

Start your own checking account for your business

In the beginning of your business there will be some expenses for permits, licenses, stationery, or samples of products. Set up a separate checking account for these items, instead of using your own personal checking account. Open a checking account in the name of your business; for example, one catalog owner uses The Tools Catalog account. Use your business account to pay all expenses for your business; do not pay for any personal expenses, including your shoe repair or theater tickets, with this account. Keep a record of all your deposits into your account and invoices for the payment you make in the account. In order to avoid problems, keep your personal finances separate from your business finances.

Hire an accountant to keep your taxes straight

In the beginning of your business take the time and effort to search for an accountant to help you set up a system to record your financial affairs of your business. There are simply four basic transactions for your business: cash receipts, cash payments, purchases, and sales for your business. Once your system is developed to handle these basic transactions, you will have all the information necessary to show you profit in your business. You will be required to pay taxes only on the profits of your business. Profits will be discussed later in this book, but it is the difference between your total revenue or sales less your expenses for your business.

Once your accountant has set up a system to handle your transactions, keep your records up to date by doing the entries daily or weekly. Avoid the habit of delaying your accounting—records might get lost, recorded twice, or mishandled due to the lack of a regular accounting schedule. Do your bank statement reconciliation as soon as possible after receiving it.

Do you need a computer in your business?

This is one of the most popular questions in my home-based seminar. The answer is simple—it depends on the individual situation. If you have extensive computer equipment at home and understand how computerized information can help you in the business, by all means use it. However, if you lack computer skills and have little interest in using a computer, do not let this stop you from starting the business. You can still learn the essentials, using this book, to start a catalog marketing business. I recommend taking a beginner computer course at your local high school or junior or community college to get the ground floor information on the computer, including keyboard training, and how it can help a small business grow and develop. The success of your catalog business will be based on information and testing, and a computer can give you access to this important information.

Avoid isolating yourself

Some home business owners spend so much time organizing their work space that they spend all their time there without being around people to get new ideas. A New Hampshire mail order owner joined a woman's professional group to socialize and get new ideas for selling and marketing; she also enjoys the techniques and ideas presented by the weekly speakers. Remember, you're in charge. Set up your routine so you can stay fresh and creative.

First impressions count— get quality stationery

In the beginning days of your business, you will be sending out letters requesting samples of products, requesting prices, and asking for information on renting mailing lists. Print up some quality stationery and envelopes with your name, address, telephone, and fax number, so you can look professional and increase your chances of receiving this important information. You can create a sophisticated and professional impression with quality stationery and envelopes by utilizing the services of a quick-print shop. Remember, your customers, suppliers, associates will not see your office space, but they will make decisions about you based on the quality of your stationery. One catalog owner from Pennsylvania tried to get information for her business without professional stationery, and the responses were poor. Once she printed 100 copies of quality stationery and envelopes and used them in her correspondence, the responses were quicker and much more complete. This same quality consciousness is important in your catalogs as well; the higher the quality of your mailings, the higher the responses, and your success will result from a favorable response from your potential customers.

Set guidelines with other family members

Organizing your office at home is important, but you must also get the cooperation from other members of your household or family to give you the space, and quiet, and time to concentrate on your catalog business. For example, one catalog owner in Minnesota found she could never get started on her priorities because her friends wanted her to join them for extended lunches or mall shopping trips. After initially giving in to their requests, she laid down the guidelines for her friends, "I really enjoy your company, but I have committed myself to getting my catalog business started, and I cannot attend these weekly lunches and shopping trips." Her friends were startled initially but now understand her situation, and their friendship still remains. Remember, you control your actions and your time management. Do the things necessary to succeed. You might be able to get help from your family members by getting them involved. There is no time to lose to win in your business.

Summary

Many successful catalogs were started right on the kitchen table at home. A spare room can be an important starter for your business. Get a comfortable desk and chair and file cabinets. Design your office space for efficiency, using good lighting and cheery colors for walls in your working area. Go to your office regularly to make it part of your lifestyle. Carefully check your insurance and legal coverage for your business. Get the necessary licenses and permits. Obtain accounting help; use a computer if you find one helpful. Choose the best business organization for you, and organize your business for productivity, and remember that quality stationery pays off. Set guidelines to others. You have now built the solid foundation to turn your catalog into a winning business.

3

Why do people buy from a catalog?

This may be the most important chapter in this book because once you determine why people buy from catalogs, and then deliver a well-planned catalog with carefully selected products, packaged just right with a hard-hitting creative wallop, you can become victorious in this business. Too often, catalog owners, and at last count there are over 9000 of them, simply assume they know why people buy from catalogs without determining the real reason that people buy from catalogs today.

People want convenience

Your well-planned, carefully focused catalog offers convenience for your customers by delivering your latest catalog directly to their mail boxes. The convenience principle includes the opportunity given the customer to browse your catalog and check off products and services of interest, and then offer a toll-free telephone number and order card to buy from you. Your catalog telephone number will give your customers the added convenience of calling you for placement of their orders, but more important, your customer can ask you questions; once questions are successfully answered, an order can then be placed with you. The telephone order and inquiries are essential to build your catalog marketing business. For example, L. L. Bean will receive over 100,000 calls on the Monday after Thanksgiving from customers doing their Christmas shopping. Calls to this catalog company will be serviced fully during the shopping season. Give as many reasons as you can why you can offer your customers the convenience they need to order from you. The easier it will be to order and do business with you, the more orders you will receive.

People buy because a product meets their lifestyle needs

The career woman wants products and services to help her reach her career goals at work. These products include books, tapes, seminars, and magazines and newsletters as well as catalog products to succeed in a very difficult career field. An example is the Blair Mail Order company in Pennsylvania, which sells men's trousers to people who want to save money. Blair sells two trousers for $20 and a simple dress for as low as $25. Their huge mailing list of 17 million customers speaks for itself, people buy because they get satisfaction from buying from Blair. A catalog marketing firm in New Hampshire sells sewing kits to its customers, which help them in two ways: the kit gives them something to do in their spare time and offers an opportunity to save money. Each business is successful because its owner knows the lifestyle and needs of customers or potential customers and then delivers them the best catalog possible.

People buy based on basic human motives

Your customers will buy your product once they are convinced you offer something to solve their psychological, physiological, social, and creative needs. They want to know how the products you are marketing by catalog can help them:

____ Become more successful

____ Become important to others

____ Become respected in a specific field

____ Become more creative

____ Become more likable to others

____ Become a leader at work

____ Become more attractive

____ Become a good conversationalist

___ Become the "life of the party"

___ Become financially secure

___ Become more respected by family

___ Become a business owner

___ Become a successful purchaser of goods

___ Become a home owner

___ Become slimmer and more appealing

___ Become interested and help others

___ Become an extensive traveler

How will these basic human motives apply to your products or services? Check the ones which are important to you. Note which ones apply to your product, you can then focus on what strategy to use to get your potential customers to buy from you. For example, one catalog marketing owner from New York sells how-to small business, entrepreneur publications and tapes for people all over the country. The basic buying motives for his products would be the motive to want to start one's own business, become financially secure, become more interesting, and grow into a leader at work. His business is growing more and more each year because he's presenting his products directly to this group of customers with these motives in mind. Your customers will buy from you when their buying motives are fully considered in your catalog.

People buy because of their expectations

Once your catalog is read, marked up, and discussed within the house or organization, a decision is made about your catalog offer. The decision might be no. The decision might be a maybe, but not now. The decision might be yes, and the customer will send you the order. This is the most important goal for every catalog owner: to put together a catalog marketing program that will result in the most sales possible. In order to do this, everything must be right, from the selection of products to pricing to customer service.

Your customer has decided your product can meet his or her needs and expectations and therefore sends you a check or money order or credit card authorization. Your job now will be to do everything possible to fulfill the confidence your customer showed in you. Work with all your might to fulfill your customer's expectations and sell more products in the future.

People buy when the timing is right

The catalog which arrives in time for the Christmas gift buying season will have a far better chance to sell than the catalog which arrives after the season is over. People buy all year long, so your catalog should try to get the order from the cold and wet January days to the hot July days to the frosty December days. Try to develop a "sense of urgency" within your potential customers to get them to buy today. Show why it's important to send that order out today. Studies in mail order and catalog buying behavior show that most sales are the result of convincing your customer to order now. The people who hesitate might buy later, but often do not, and the people who say "no" usually do not buy. Ask for the order strongly on the first presentation, and get the order right now.

An interesting thing happened to me a few weeks ago, which sometimes happens in this business. I have been in mail order for almost 20 years; I started selling a manual on how to start a newsletter, and the price was $10. Two weeks ago I received a letter in which the buyer wanted to purchase a manual, and he mentioned he misplaced the order card but included my original sales letter. Once I had a chance to review the letter, I discovered that it was sent to the customer almost 14 years ago. The customer might have misplaced the order card but was organized enough to find the letter to send the order to me. In this business, your catalog will start a buying process within the customer, and your goal will be to get the order right now and not later.

People buy because they believe in you

Trust in the cement which holds the catalog marketing business together. When that catalog reader, the senior citizen from Seattle, Washington, reviews your catalog, or the young man from Vermont sends you that order, the real reason is because he or she believes in you. The readers believe you have those products or services, and that you will ship them when you stated in your terms, and that you will give them the full guarantee and accept a return of those products or services for their full purchase price if the customers are unsatisfied in any way. Your complete honesty to follow up on your promises, or make a good faith effort to do so, will be essential to your success in the catalog business.

People buy from you because you're different

This is where you can succeed and beat your competition by having a slight edge on them, to look better in your customers' eyes. Your potential customers spend a lot of time reviewing other catalogs and looking in stores. Your potential customers know a great deal about your products, prices, benefits, and terms. When you send out a catalog with products similar to your competition, with essentially the same prices and terms, it will be difficult to get the sale. By changing the approach and doing it a little differently you can succeed. I like the quote from Joe Sugarman, a mail order professional, who started from his kitchen table, and produces catalogs to sell to millions all over the country and the world: "...to break into the mail order business, is the ability to innovate or do something different, you create a very powerful success force. The secret is *don't copy*. You succeed when you innovate." Keep these words in mind in your business. Remember, every product or service has a place in the sun. Each product can grow and develop when it is presented in an attractive manner. Some ways to make your product look attractive, appealing, and unique are: show the product in action, stress benefits which appeal to your consumers, give many facts and vital information about the product or service, make your product easy to purchase, give your consumers new ideas about how they could benefit from your product, and show the product in a different manner. Do it differently.

People buy because of flexibility and choice

Your catalog readers will buy when you present to them a variety of choices to meet their needs. A catalog marketing owner sells advertising specialties such as key chains, pens, coffee holders, jack knives, clips, imprinted golf balls, matches, rulers, nail clippers, money clips, and lighters to independent businesses such as banks, real estate agents, car dealers, insurance agents, cleaning companies, and restaurants. Her business is growing because it offers such a wide assortment and is very flexible offering special terms for larger orders. People enjoy an opportunity to review your product over and over again, so they can purchase it for themselves or offer it as a gift for a friend or family member.

People buy for excitement

Many consumers order for the sheer thrill of visualizing in their minds what the product will look like in package form, how it will help them in their lives. In order to focus on the consumers who want the thrill of buying by mail, you need to think about making your product look attractive and tell them the benefits fully so they will buy from you.

People buy because your product appealed to them

People will buy only when they feel your product or service suits them. You cannot sell a product unless people want it. Each time someone orders a product from you this is a victory. Your job will be to position or present your product to get your consumers to remember it, think about it, and finally buy it.

People buy because they can afford it

Good catalog marketing is matching the product to the consumer who has the money or the purchasing power such as credit cards, money in the bank, or access to the money needed to buy your product. The consumer may not have enough money in cash but can use a credit card to make the purchase from you. Send your catalog to people with the purchasing power to buy.

People buy because they expect good values from your product or service

Your catalog will be read by your consumer at leisure, and will be reviewed to see whether it has any interest or not. Your offer includes your product, price, terms, bonuses, guarantees, and instructions on how to order. When your offer is well planned and presented professionally you increase your chances to get at least a small order from the consumer. Once you get the order, follow up with personal customer service so you can get the consumers to buy again with a larger order.

People buy because they sense your excitement and enthusiasm

The way you present your products and the words you use to describe how your products can benefit the consumer will be important elements to close the sale with your important consumer. Customers want to buy from someone who knows the product and business and is willing to serve their needs. Follow through by getting so involved people will be aware of it and respond positively to you. Get into your business fully. I have a quote taped on my computer which reads *If you're in something, get into it. If you're not in it, get out.*

People buy because they are willing to make a single purchase

The order came to you, a single order for only $29.99, but it's very important because the customer read your offer and decided to choose you as her retail store of the catalog world. Your challenge will be to follow up with the order, give excellent service, and include your latest catalog with the order to get the "bounce back" sale once the customer is satisfied. This is the most important challenge for you as a catalog marketing owner, to keep selling, but once you get a customer, turn him or her into a customer for life. Your success will depend upon it.

People buy because you know the market

Successful companies pride themselves on the fact they not only know their products but they know the people or market who buys from them. In order to get to know their market, companies conduct marketing research to learn about customer's opinions, interests, and lifestyles. For example, a Massachusetts catalog marketing company knew there were 10 million personal computer programmers worldwide and set a strategy to reach this market. For 10 full years the company sold computer specialty tool and software packages to this market. The company grew so fast that it opened offices in Germany and Italy to serve the European market. The catalog is called *The Programmers Shops* and offers many products produced by computer companies. The catalog was started six years ago and continues to grow year after year; one of the major reasons that it succeeded was the ability of the company to learn the needs of the market, and once that market was fully satisfied, to move on to other markets. The company is now looking to market its products and direct its catalog to include engineers, mathematicians, and statisticians. The company found that the number of engineers who use a personal computer for their work has increased over 10 times during the past five years. The company is the only source for over half the products sold in its catalog.

Become an expert on how your product is used

Large companies test the uses for their products or services by doing a focus group, which is getting a cross-section of all your potential consumers and letting them fully examine your product and give you the necessary feedback so you can match your product to the right customer. For example, let's say you want to do a catalog on toys for children, to get important marketing data, you could convene a focus group, whereby you invite white, black, Hispanic, Asian, and Native American children to attend. Permit the children to use the toys, and as they begin to play with the toys focus on how they play with each toy, how long they play with it before putting it down, whether they play with the toy on the ground, hold it, or run it along the walls. Each use for your product can be highlighted in your catalog copy to increase potential sales, so the more you know about your product users, the better chances of increased sales. You now become an expert on your product.

When you are selling software packages to engineers, it might be interesting to call a number of engineers to ask them how the programs are being used; perhaps they even found some uses for your products which you never expected. Take the time to measure the use of your product on a regular basis.

Become an expert on consumer behavior

Successful catalog owners know that the customer has needs, and when these needs are met a sale will result. All sales are the result of going through a process. This process starts when the consumer receives the catalog in the mailbox. Unfortunately it is not the only catalog or mail order offering the consumer will receive that day. The competition is intense. In order for you to get the order everything must be correct, from the product, price, and ease of ordering to how attractive you make your product look.

One of my most popular questions in my catalog marketing seminars is, "How can you learn consumer behavior?" The answer is a simple one: by testing. Keep testing your product selection, pricing, format, special sales, and incentives until you get an offer which works for you. We will discuss testing in more detail later in the book. Testing will be the difference between success and failure in this business. The successful people continue to test.

Get your consumer interested in your product

A key goal is to get your potential customers interested in your product or service. Once they pick up your catalog you must use those first few minutes to lock their interest and get them fully involved in your presentation. A catalog marketer of toys shows the children playing with the toys inside as well as outside the house, another catalog on clothing shows models wearing the latest selection of fall and winter clothing. You are selling, and it will be up to you to sell the benefits of your product by making it look as good as possible.

One very successful hi-tech toy product catalog marketer, Joe Sugarman, the producer of the *Products Which Think* catalog, uses the principle of getting the reader of the catalog involved by giving as much information as possible about the product, including facts and figures. He gives the size, weight, capacity, length of life, and other facts. Sugarman is able to present this important information because he uses the products himself before he writes the copy for them in the catalog. He tries to become an expert. Sugarman feels the more information he can offer the reader, the better chance the potential customer will buy from him. Sugarman also runs advertisements in large circulation newspapers and magazines, and, once he finds a successful advertisement, he then puts it into his next catalog. Sugarman feels catalog marketing success is the result of examining products and then, once you find a real good one, to do the necessary catalog marketing to make it a winner.

Keep a file on ideas to help sell the potential customer

As you read this book, you will learn some new ways to sell to your customers; when you come up with an idea, put it into your idea file. For example, the idea file might include a new product idea, how to motivate a potential customer, benefits of your product, a new layout idea, a copy of an advertisement which keeps running in national magazines, an idea for a coupon or rebate promotion, or any article or research on catalog marketing which can help you. Review your file often, and try to incorporate these ideas into your business. I know one catalog marketer who keeps a section of his file cabinet just for ideas to help him in his catalog business. You can do the same.

Determine who is the decision maker for your products

Who will make the decision to say "yes" or "no" to your offer? Every successful catalog marketer must spend some important time and effort on this important question. In your own mind, follow your catalog to the prospect's home or place of business; once it is taken from the mailbox, imagine who will receive it, how it will be read and handled, and what the final decision will be on the fate of the catalog. When the catalog is sent to Joe Jones, will he send the check out right away or charge the purchase to his credit card? Or will he discuss the purchase with his wife or significant other before a purchasing decision is made of your product or service? In marketing, the people who determine whether the product or service is purchased is effected by the gatekeeper, the person in the family, such as the wife, husband, mother, father, or grandparent who will encourage or discourage the purchase. In the business environment, the gatekeeper might be the manager of the department, who is in charge of approval of purchases for the department, or it might be the purchasing agent who will make the decision about your product. The purchasing agent might look even more carefully into the price, specifications, guarantees, discounts, and special offers and therefore become an important consideration in your strategies.

Summary

People want the convenience of buying by catalog. Your catalog business should consider your consumer's lifestyle needs. People have expectations based on the way you present your products and services, and you must consider and service these important expectations. Timing is everything in the catalog business. Your prospects send in their order card because they believe in you and in your products. People buy from you because of your excitement and enthusiasm seen through your catalog presentation. You succeed when you appeal directly to your prospects. Show your prospects how the product or service can be used. Know the process of making a purchase by mail order. Know your market and your decision makers. Keep a file on your ideas to keep up with the changes in the field.

4

Selecting your product or service

One of the most important and perplexing questions for home-based catalog business owners, and one of the popular questions in seminars is simply: What product or line of products should I choose for my catalog business? The answer is not a simple one, but my response is a simple, quick one: Choose something you like and know a lot about or simply are very interested in. To further explore possible product and service ideas, take a close look at your hobbies, the books or periodicals you read; how you spend your spare time will give you information on what product you should choose for your business. Notice I am talking about a single product or a single service in the beginning of your product selection process. Thinking about a line of products dilutes the process and makes it much more difficult to make a final decision. By choosing a single product, called a "lead product," you gain much needed knowledge about the product, how it is made, features, benefits, and extra uses of product, and all this information will help you market the product more successfully.

Start small and focus on one product at a time. Take the example of Stan in New Hampshire, an accountant by day but an avid golfer at night and on weekends. Stan found a putting club which helped his putting game and was so enthusiastic about it, he told all his golfing friends, neighbors, and associates at work. Finally, an associate at work remarked, "Stan why don't you sell this product by mail order? It sure sounds like a winner." Stan decided to purchase some of these clubs, and he also purchased a small advertisement in a golf magazine. The response was favorable, and once he received a letter for more information, Stan forwarded a sales letter and a brochure showing a photo of the club, additional information, and an order card. This is what is called two-step marketing, which means your advertisement describes the benefits of the product in the small space advertisement, and once the prospect requests more, additional information is sent to close the sale. The value of the two-step method is that you get a chance to see how many people respond and you get a chance to build your own house list, people who expressed an interest in your product or service and know you. Stan is now working on a line of golf products, including golf clothing, books, and additional clubs. Successful catalog marketers start with one product and they move on to a line of products over time.

A writer from California, Betty, was interested in self-development and received real joy in helping others reach their goals at work and in business. Betty decided to write a manual on how to start a word processing business, and like Stan, ran an advertisement in a business opportunity magazine to target her market; she sold over a thousand manuals during the next year using this method. Once she established this first success, she built on it by producing additional manuals and reports. Betty found that her house list was over 4000 names of people who purchased from her or asked for more information (these people are called "inquiries" in the catalog business). Both Stan and Betty started slow and small; once their lead products were developed and they had gathered a great deal of information by marketing in small-space advertisements, they had built a list to lead the way into the catalog marketing business. An excellent way to get into the catalog business is to choose a product or service you really believe in, get as much information about it as possible, and even market it yourself, and then you have the information you need to succeed in this business.

Do you hold all rights or simply buy and resell the products?

The examples given earlier show both methods of selling: Stan simply bought the putting club and resold it, and Betty produced the manual on her own and resold it herself, therefore opening up the door to larger profits for the future. There are advantages to both methods. When you produce the product yourself, you must give consideration to the time and effort you must give to the research and development and production time of your products. Some catalog marketers develop a catalog which has both products or services they produce and others which they purchase to resell. A software catalog marketer offers a catalog in which the owner controls about 75 percent of the products, which simply means you can only buy these products from her company. A business books catalog is offered by Susan, a teacher in New Jersey, and it offers books, manuals, and reports for small to medium-size businesses, and all publications are produced and owned by her. Try to avoid permitting the owning versus buying for resale decision to affect your initial selection of your product or service for your catalog. Notice I said product, singular, and service, not services—start small with one product and build on from there to success.

Choose a product which relates to your interests

Fran from New Mexico decided to do a catalog on personal computers because she has worked with computers for over 20 years and knows the field inside out. A catalog marketer from Illinois spent 12 years in the shipping and receiving business, and knew the products and services needed to run a successful shipping supply specialists catalog business. He is now running his own catalog marketing business selling envelopes, staplers, shipping bags, twine, tape, strapping, and other shipping products. A bank servicing New England reviewed all the products and services and decided a catalog offering all the services together would provide its customers and prospects with much needed information about such things as bank service cards, checking accounts, student services, retirement accounts, home equity credit, and travel services. See Fig. 4-1 below. Another family from New Jersey sold paper, and their real interest was in paper for the business office, especially colored stationery which could be put into the copy machine to reproduce a sales letter or a special memorandum. Once the catalog was sent out, the readers were requested to send for a sample kit, for a price of $1, to see the sample products first hand, to increase the chance of the products being sold. All these catalogs were developed because the catalog marketer had an interest and understanding of the prod-

Figure 4-1. Many catalog marketers featuring their services are finding that their customers are willing to read, compare, and buy.

ucts or services. Choose a product which excites you, stirs a passion within you, something you can talk about to others, something which will hold your interest each year from January to December, something which you feel so positive about you can sell to others. Talking about a product such as a golf club, book, or software is one thing, but being able to sell it is another. In catalog marketing nothing happens until a sale is made, so your enthusiasm is extremely important, and stressing how the product will benefit the user or buyer is essential to success.

Your hobby might be your best product or service

One future catalog marketer, Paul from Georgia, has been interested in coins all his life; he joined with a number of other coin collectors in the Atlanta area and will be mailing out a catalog on coins this summer. Tom from Tennessee has been interested in antique Model T Fords for over 30 years and was recently elected president of his local club. Tom decided to develop a catalog to sell parts for these antique automobiles, and the catalog which goes out three times each year includes seat covers, books, and many other products relating to this important hobby. Corrienne is interested in physical fitness, and many of her family and friends told her to start a business to sell her information to others about fitness and health. Corrienne made a list of all the books, products, and clothing she felt were essential to her success in fitness, and the result was a potential catalog of her own. Corrienne handed out the first few copies to the people in her exercise class at the local high school, and she plans to show the book when she speaks on the local talk cable television program. Make a list of the hobbies or interests you have right now, along with interests and sports in which you participated in the past, e.g., skiing, antiques, photography.

Interest/Hobbies

_____   _____

_____   _____

_____   _____

Earlier in the book, I mentioned the catalog owner who learned much by setting up her own wedding. The research which went into organizing the affair gave her the motivation and impetus to start her own bridal catalog. Knowing a hobby or field extremely well is a solid foundation on which to build a successful catalog business. You will return to this section of the book when the final decision is made on your product or service.

What is the best possible product or service?

There is plenty of competition in the catalog marketing business, so to compete successfully, try to choose the product or service which will succeed for you. Successful marketers know that products are made for people, and people are not made for the products. Choose a product which fulfills a need, and people will buy over and over again. It is very expensive to make the first sale, and your profits will be made on the repeat sales you make over and over again. Here is a list of the catalog superstar product for the nineties:

- A high-quality product or service
- A unique product

- A product not available at stores
- A product that can be used by a broad section of the population
- A product that will be used up and will require another purchase, e.g., computer paper, office supplies, solutions to a problem
- A product easy to store
- A product easy to mail
- A product that offers many benefits which you can use in your selling activities
- A product you can sell at 3 to 4 times your cost, to earn a profit
- An attractive product with modern features, something your customer will be proud to show off to others
- A product that does not break or melt and is easy to install
- A product needed by a special group of people or businesses
- A product used by young, middle age, and older people
- A product, either very simple or complex, which people will buy by mail

Use the guidelines when you choose your initial product or service. Follow up by selling the product or service over again when it is used up, or send along with the other products your carefully planned catalog showing your full line of products. All the above characteristics are important, none more important than selecting a quality product or service, since this is the basic foundation which everything else is built upon. As important as having a quality product is, to sell the product successfully it must have features and benefits which offer results which people can readily see and therefore buy.

Your own list of possible products or services

Numerous products and services can be sold and marketed by catalog, from office supplies, to software for the computer, to Christmas trees, to products which can help people with arthritis, to baby care products. Here is a basic list to help you get started in your selection process. Included in Appendix B is a separate list for your convenience.

Some Catalog Product or Service Ideas

Antiques and reproductions
Art supplies and equipment
Financial services
Collection services
Automobile parts and accessories
Archery supplies
1950s memorabilia
Baby care products
Unique knitted goods
Bird feeders and houses
Collection services
Health and fitness products
Children's books
Camcorders
Computer supplies, software
Doll making kits
Catalog listing catalogs
Fire safety equipment
Children's gifts
Wicker furniture
Native American art and crafts
Maps
Photography supplies
Wallets and purse
Telephone and answering machines
Sports equipment
Tools

Flower seeds and bulbs
Toys
Quality processes supplies
Scuba diving supplies
Wheelchair transporters
Water purifiers
Weather vanes
Security systems
Inspirational tapes and videos
Correspondence courses
Books on tape
Large-print books
Camping supplies
Customer relations manuals
Energy conservation products
Salt-free foods
Gardening supplies and equipment
General gifts
Health care supplies
Left-handed merchandise
Ostomy supplies
Catalog on newsletters
Ties
VCRs
Electronic toys and games
Chain earrings
Books on travel information
Vitamins

This is only a small sample of potential products or services you can sell in your catalog marketing program. Check off any product or service ideas which appeal to you; remember, at this stage you are not making a final decision, you are just getting ideas for your business. Your choice of product can be something which relates to your job, your education, your hobby, or something in which you have an interest.

Keep searching for new product or service ideas

Ideas are all around you, from the moment you get up in the morning to seconds before you fall asleep at night. Many magazines present new products for their readers, and newsletters also feature products and services which will be of interest to their readership. Order products from catalogs for ideas. Keep a file of new product and service ideas, and when you find a new one, in a magazine for example, make a copy of that page and insert it into your "New Products" file for future use. Some catalog marketers attend trade shows and give their business card out to suppliers. Gift shows and household products shows are also a good way to get a first time view of new products and services. These shows offer free information about products and prices. Read all the information you can get about a product and then try the product yourself if possible. Nothing replaces your own experience in using the product or service. You would never think about purchasing a car unless you took the time to look under the hood, check the important parts to the car, and take it for a trial ride. Nothing can take the place of getting involved with your potential product or service.

Get as much information as possible about who makes your product and who sells it

Who makes your product? How is the product distributed? Can you buy your product from the manufacturer? What discount will you receive when you buy the product? You might get this information from the manufacturer at the trade show, but the reference librarian at your local or regional library will have a list of manufacturers, or a manufacturers directory to give you all the information you need to contact the manufacturer for more information. When you write to the manufacturer, make certain your letter is on your business letterhead and is typewritten, so you give a professional impression that you are serious about selecting their product or service. Keep a supplier's file, include in it a copy of your letter and all correspondence you send out, so it will be easier to respond to the manufacturer in the future.

Get to know what other people are selling, by looking for the product at various stores, including specialty stores at local and regional malls. When you find a product easily purchased in stores, it will not have the appeal to your potential customers that a unique product which cannot be found in local stores and malls will. Review the catalogs and direct mail offers you receive in your mailboxes at home and at work. Are any of the catalogs offering your products or products similar to your idea? Many catalog marketing owners request other businesses to send their catalogs to give them ideas about products and services so they can learn how these items are presented and what appeals are used in the catalog presentation. Become a catalog collector in this business. One idea is worth a potential thousand dollars. Buy some products from other catalog marketers to see their products, evaluate their value for price, and learn their customer relations skills. Did they sell you what they promised? Did they ship it promptly? Did they fix it or give you an allowance when it was broken in shipment? Did they follow up with another catalog or offer once you purchased the product? Nothing takes the place of being a customer yourself. I ask all catalog seminar attendees to purchase as many products as possible just to get an important "feel" and understanding of the business.

Research your competition

Avoid the embarrassment and the costly mistake of the writer who developed a newsletter on various French wines. After he had written his first issue and mailed out the sales letters to sell the newsletter subscriptions, he learned that there were already three newsletters of this type in circulation. This writer would have saved time, money, and effort if he took the time to research his competition. You can do this in your catalog business.

To find out if any others are selling your idea, let's say it is Native American arts and crafts by catalog, make a trip to the reference librarian at your local or regional library. I say "regional" because too often the local library may lack the reference books, which can be stocked more easily by the better-funded regional library or the library at your local college or university. Ask for the *Catalog on Catalogs* (P.O. Box 6590, Silver Spring, MD 20916-6590), a publication which gives a comprehensive listing of businesses which sell by catalog and what product or services they sell. You might want to write to the businesses listed in this reference book, especially the ones selling products or services which you are interested in marketing. By getting a chance to review their catalogs you get a chance to see products, prices, terms of sales, freight costs, and the size of their catalogs. You get to know who you will be competing with once you start your business. Another important reference book, available at your library reference section, is the *Catalog Handbook* (1020 N. Broadway, Milwaukee, WS 53202) which lists in one place thousands of major business firms, organizations, suppliers and service firms, associations, seminars, courses, consultants, artists, writers, and prominent people in the direct marketing field. An important section in this directory is the listing of businesses that use direct marketing which shows what percentage is used for selling by magazines and what percentage by catalog. Many businesses use both magazines and catalogs to get the maximum sales for their products and services. Another important feature of this directory is that it offers a free—yes, free—listing of your business, its address, and a brief description of your company and its products or services. This listing will give you an opportunity to get mail from various people in the field and to find out what is offered in the field for your business.

Just because there is competition in a particular product field does not mean you should decide to choose another product. You might want to research the product even more to determine the amount of competition and the quality of the competition. Answer questions such as: Who is the competition? What do they offer? How often do they advertise? How often do they send out their catalog? Do they have good customer relations skills? Do they have an extensive line of products? For example, do they sell a complete line of Native American arts and crafts or do they sell just a few products of art and then feature unrelated items, confusing the catalog prospect? Carefully planned catalogs will sell better than a catalog trying to sell many unrelated items together. Take the time to see what the competition is doing, and then do your own catalog better.

To specialize or not to specialize is the question

Some people reading this book have a business or a home-based business already, and they have some experience in selling certain products already; it would be very tempting to put all the products together, whether they relate to one another or not. Don't fall into this trap. Native American art and crafts do not relate to fax machines. Specialize in one area, and give the catalog prospect your best products which relate to one another. The fax machines could be sold along with copy machines and copy machine paper. The arts and crafts could be sold with arts and crafts supplies for a complete offering. Just as when you go into a store, when you shop by catalog you will stay longer when it is full of merchandise, and you will probably buy something when there is a wide assortment. Specialize and give as wide an assortment as possible.

Decision time is here

Based on what has been discussed in this chapter, I want you now to choose a product or service to which you feel a sense of commitment, in which you believe, and which you will sell energetically for 12 months, 365 days a year. In the next chapter we will discuss taking the product and building a bridge to the market or the customer of your product. Go back to page 37 if you need some product or service ideas.

Product or Service Decision

_____   _____

_____   _____

Summary

Start small by choosing one product or service. Decide whether to buy to resell or produce the product or service yourself. Focus on your interests, sports, or hobbies. Review the elements of the successful mail order product or service. Review the list of products given in this chapter. Search for products in catalogs, trade shows, and specialty and gift shows, and contact manufacturers on full details. Research your competition. Make a final decision on your product or service. Now let's move on to the bridge to connect to your consumer.

5

Building a bridge to your customer

In the last chapter you focused on choosing a product or service which will be the important spark to build your catalog marketing business. From your short list you selected a product to offer and sell to your potential customers. Now ask yourself who can use or buy your product: You need customers to succeed. A market is a particular group of people with specific needs and desires and purchasing power. *Market* is too broad a term in direct marketing or catalog marketing; successful marketers focus on a *target market* such as software engineers, business owners, carpenters, attorneys, brides, elementary school teachers, bankers, pilots, college students, gift shop owners, certified public accountants, jewelry stores, and nurses. Now your success in the catalog marketing business will depend upon your ability to build this bridge between the product or products you selected to your target market. You have no time to lose because the target market is being served by other catalogs and direct marketing firms right now. Your bridge connecting your product and your target market must be very strong with a reinforced foundation to get your product or service to your important target market. This foundation, the imaginary bridge, is your strategy, and this will become the cornerstone of your success. In my marketing semi-nars I call this "connecting" with your customer. Your chief objective is to bring them together. You become an important "match-maker" bringing your carefully researched product to your market. For example, an institute concerned about the quality of work life in America sells information on productivity in the form of books, research reports, studies by catalog to a market which is worldwide. A home-based catalog marketer from Massachusetts sells knitting yarns, patterns, and accessories all over the United States and Canada. A Brooklyn-based catalog marketer of eyeglasses sells to a ready market of buyers in the United States and Canada. A museum in New England sells their museum reproductions in their gift catalog. A gourmet foods company in Illinois sells meats, fruits, and cheeses by catalog. A New Mexico gift shop sells to a national association. Your product has a unique and specialized market for you to prospect and eventually mine; there are hundreds, even thousands, of markets.

Get to know your market fully

In your business, try to think and act just like a salesperson. Get to know your target market fully in order to sell more successfully. Who is he or she? Where does this individual live? What is his or her marital status? How much does this person earn? What is her or his job? These questions are important to establishing the demographics of your market, which means the tangible specifics of your customer such as sex, race, geographical location, and income. These statistics become extremely important to you because if you're selling to high-income people you can offer products of a higher quality and price than if you offered it to a market with a lower-income level. Age can affect what products are purchased as well. An 18-year-old first-year student in college will be interested in selecting products or services to meet his or her needs such as educational and hobby materials, and videos for the VCR. This same person 8 to 10 years later, recently married and working, will be interested in many other products such as furniture, insurance, and a home. Age, income, and marital status have important influences on what is purchased. Below you will find a listing of basic demographics.

Demographics

Age	Ages of children living at home
Income	Occupation

Sex	Spouse's occupation
Marital status	Credit card usage
Home ownership	Geography
Race	Education

Where you live can be very important for your catalog business by targeting customers living in affluent communities. For example one large mail order company sends their catalog to every family in Weston, Massachusetts, for that very reason.

Learn how your customers live

Extent your knowledge of your market beyond knowing how much Corrienne Smith earns in her accounting position with a San Francisco advertising agency and how much she uses her credit card. What are her interests, attitudes, opinions? Is she a collector of books, videos, or antiques? How much time does she spend each week with her dog? How important is exercise, nutrition, and physical fitness to Corrienne? How many hours per week will she view cable television versus network television? Lifestyles and interests open up many product and market choices. For example, if Corrienne Smith will spend 2 hours daily with her pet dog, she may also be interested in pet supplies, books, and accessories. Your well-planned pet supplies and accessories catalog will find a more receptive reader in Corrienne than if it is sent to her brother in Minneapolis who is allergic to and dislikes pets. If Corrienne spends many hours per week jogging at the health club, she would be much more interested in products and services related to fitness and nutrition. Your products and services must service the needs of this important target market.

Below you will find a listing of various lifestyles and interests which are so important in your marketing strategies and activities. Try to look at the large picture of your product and the market it seeks.

Available Selections: Lifestyles and Interests

Art, antique collecting	Automotive work
Bible, devotional reading	Bicycling frequently
Boating, sailing	Book reading
Cable T.V. viewing	Camping, hiking
C.B. radio	Collectibles, collections
Community, civic events	Crafts

Cultural, art events

Fashion clothing

Foreign travel

Gardening (renters)

Gourmet cooking, fine foods

Health foods, vitamins

Home video games

Household pets (dogs, cats, etc.)

Money-making opportunities

Needlework, knitting

Personal, home computer

Physical fitness, exercise

Recreational vehicles, 4-wheel drive

Science fiction

Self-improvement

Sewing, needlework

Stamps, coin collecting

Stocks, bond investment

Tennis frequently

Watching sports on TV

Electronics

Fishing frequently

Gardening (homeowners)

Golf

Grandchildren

Home furnishing, decorating

Home workshop

Hunting shooting

Motorcycles

Our nation's heritage

Photography

Real estate investments

Running, jogging

Science, new technology

Sewing

Snow skiing frequently

Stereo systems, compact disks, and tapes

Sweepstakes entrants

Videocassette recording (VCR)

Wildlife, environmental issues

Wines

You are giving a party this week to your associates at work

Trying to explain the process of establishing a line of products to sell by catalog and producing it and mailing it out is no easy assignment. It reminds me of my college instructor, Professor Hardy, talking about being a teacher. He said, "It is easier talking about it than doing it." The process of cataloging is similar to being asked by your boss to put on a party for the people in your office for having a successful year. Your boss told you to be creative, even set a theme—but the most important point is to make the party enjoyable for all. After you walk back to your office and gather your thoughts, you then take a pad of paper and go in one of the unused meeting rooms in your office. Sit down at the table; the head of the table is preferred. Now when you look at the empty chairs, they represent the employees you will be serving during your party. What would they like to do at the party? What activities seem appropriate? What theme can you develop for the party? What would they like to eat? What type of music would you offer? What type of entertainment or after-dinner speaker would work for you? The answers to these questions will make the difference between a successful party or an unsuccessful one. In the catalog business you want to take your product and position it in an attractive manner to appeal to your prospect. In the process of reading your catalog, your prospect develops a mood which will influence him or her to take the time and effort to fill out the order card and send it to you. Your objective is to *sell,* yes sell, not just showcase your products or services. In order to sell, you must develop a relationship with your guests. Permit your audience to have a good time. It is difficult to be both the host and to have a good time as well. Strive to position yourself as someone genuinely interested in the welfare of the audience or your guests.

During the party you will be kind to all your guests, but you will spend more time with some guests than others. Some people have athletic or mechanical ability and prefer to work with tools and machines and to be outdoors. When you have their interests you will spend time with them. If you have an interest in working with data, or doing clerical duties, following through on others' instructions, you will have a great time talking to them. Or you might feel even more comfortable spending time and relating to people who like to inform, help, train, develop others. Giving the party and finding out what your favorite group happens to be is very similar to the important process of doing your catalog.

Visualize your business as giving an important party, setting a tone, giving a specific atmosphere, and developing this pleasing relationship by the service you give, treating your customers so well that they will become customers for life.

Cultivate the heavy users

The heavy users are people so involved in their hobby, interest, or business that they will spend a large percentage of their income to buy related products and services. Once you establish your business, these heavy users will make themselves known to you. Heavy users read your catalog and buy regularly from each one. They might order two or three times using the same catalog.

They respond to all your mailings, you space advertisements in magazines, your classified advertisements, and even to your mention of your products on a local cable show or radio show. I once sent a catalog to a heavy user from Canada who bought every product in the catalog. Cultivate these heavy users; they are essential to help you grow your business off the kitchen table to a substantial business.

Select a market you can service

Some catalog marketers become too optimistic about their ability to satisfy and service a market. For example a New England cookbook catalog marketer tried to sell 15 different cookbooks to her prospects using the two-step marketing method, running a classified advertisement and following up with the catalog. The beginning results were poor. She decided to increase her list of cookbooks to hundreds of different publications including Mexican, French, Bavarian, and Texas-style cooking, and sales increased dramatically. You can increase your product selection with the minimum cost when you select suppliers who are willing to drop-ship for you. This means you advertise in your catalog a cookbook on Mexican cooking for $25.00 plus shipping. When you get the order, you simply send a check for $12.50 plus $1.00 shipping, along with an address label giving the full name and address of the buyer to the drop shipper who will ship the cookbook directly to your buyer. Make certain you include your return address on the address label, so customers can reorder from you.

Consider many possible target markets

Be willing to look at as many markets as possible in your business. Look for a niche, a market which is small but has the income, interest, and desire to purchase your products from you. Below you will find a list of possible markets for the product or service of your choice.

Possible Markets

Accountants	Manufacturers
Bank credit card holders	Members of fitness centers
Business owners	Model T Ford owners
Buyers of inspirational books	Mutual fund investors
Chemical engineers	Physicians

Computer, VCR owners   Salespeople in computer field
Expensive jewelry buyers   Software engineers
Fax owners   Women attorneys
Gift store owners   Women executives
Handicapped

You can reach many of these markets by renting a mailing list or by advertising in a magazine or publication read by the target market. For example, if you sell supplies and accessories for fax machines, you might want to purchase a directory of fax owners, or rent a list to send your catalog to them. By placing an advertisement in a magazine such as *Popular Mechanics,* you can reach the do-it-yourself market of hundreds of thousands of readers quickly and easily. This is just a small list to get you started; a more comprehensive list is in Chapter 11 of the book.

Match your product to your market and strategy now

As we wind up this chapter I want you to match your product or service with the market or markets to which your product or service best appeals. Try to select a market which you feel you have a good rapport with, a market which has the ability to grow and develop within the next decade and well into the twenty-first century.

Products or Service	*Market(s)*
FAX supplies	FAX owners
_____	FAX service engineers
_____	_____
_____	_____

This chapter will not be complete unless you can, in a paragraph or two, describe the strategy you would like to use to succeed in this business. For example, in the party which you put on for your associates at work, what theme and strategy would you like to use to make it successful in your catalog field? As you read the book I want you to continue to come back to focus on three things: (1) your product or service, (2) your market, and (3) your strategy.

Strategy Statement

Summary

Your target market is the most important element in your business. Develop a strategy to fully connect your product to your customer. Get to know other products and their target markets in the catalog business. Demographics and psychographics help you to learn more about your market. Serving the heavy users is essential to your success. Consider all possible markets. Select a market you can service. Use the two-step marketing method. Match your product, market, and strategy together. Write out your strategy statement completely. Now let's move on to pricing your product or service.

6

Pricing your product or service

Pricing is one of the most important elements in your catalog marketing business because your customer is very price conscious and will judge your catalog based on how your product or service is priced. The price might be judged as too high or too low for the quality of your product or service. It might be judged as mid-range priced for your product, and this could hurt you because the potential customer might put your catalog aside and look at your competitors to continue the buying process. Getting the best possible price is not an easy task, but thankfully it is another element in the catalog marketing business which can be tested, changed, and retested, until you get the price which will give you the maximum orders.

The decade of the nineties has shown many mail order businesses and catalog owners moving their prices down to try to reach out for more orders, especially during the recession which started in many parts of the country in the late 1980s. Many catalog owners have offered their lead products at prices at cost or even below cost to get the customer to try the product and to become a customer for life.

Successful pricing has a lot to do with the strategy we talked about in the previous chapter—once you focus on a particular strategy, your pricing becomes an important extension of it. For example, a catalog owner selling unique New England antique desks can ask and obtain the higher price for these special products. Analyze your product or service fully before you even consider setting a price. Ask yourself what you would pay for this product if it was presented to you in catalog during the cold and snowy month of January in your home in Winona, Minnesota.

Know the role of pricing versus the extended product

Your price is part of your marketing strategy, and it is paying for more than the physical product; you are selling the extended product. Let's say your product is a personal computer which you are selling for $1999. This price must not be the most important element in your strategy, because today's difficult-to-please consumer will look at the value of the product for the price. The extended product will include the installation of the computer, the smooth running performance, the solving of problems for the consumer, the service after the sale, the warranty, and the guarantee. These are all essential for your success in the sales of the product. As one veteran catalog marketer from Hollywood stated, "Catalog sales blossom when you can present the whole product or services fully to showcase the value relative to the price. Open the heavy curtain to show the value on the center stage." This is the intangible element in marketing, to know the extended product and then communicate this extended product and benefits to your market.

Review competitors' products

Your potential customers have many catalogs on their coffee tables, on their desks at work, or in their dens, and they know the range and many prices for the products or services of interest to them. As part of their buying process, they compare prices along with the future value of the products. I know one catalog marketer in Massachusetts who sends a catalog twice a year to a mailing list of 50,000 customers and to people who request a catalog, called "inquiries," and all his products, mostly "get ahead, get rich, start your business books," are sold at the top price possible; many books are sold at $44.95. This higher-price strategy is working for him, and new products are presented each catalog issue. He also tells the people on his mailing list to buy from this catalog, or he will stop mailing it to them; the strategy is one which stresses the value of getting the catalog, and to continue it will require the receiver to buy a product. Another catalog owner in Michigan offering forms, application forms, and posters, incentive awards for personnel managers, uses just the opposite strategy for pricing. She uses the low-end pricing method, which sells the products at the lowest price possible to build up her catalog list, obtaining sales based on quantity selling to medium-size and small businesses. Choose a price which will make your product attractive to the consumer and still make a profit for you.

Demand will affect your price

The *demand* is the economic term to indicate the number of people in your target market who have the willingness and the money or the credit necessary to buy your product. Both the willingness and the money are necessary in order to create the demand. For example, too often catalog marketers send their freshly printed catalogs to a list of doctors primarily because they are one of the highest income groups of any occupation; these marketers find their results are less then they expected. Why? Doctors are very selective in their purchasing decisions and will only buy when they feel the quality, benefits, and features of the product will meet their lifestyle and their needs. When a product or line of products fails to meet these requirements, the order is delayed or not placed. To determine your demand for your product, get to know your target market even more; look at the present economic conditions, determine where your consumer is living (in the city? in the South? in the West?), in what income group he or she is, and what his or her specific occupation is. Keep testing to obtain the price with the best demand for your product.

The lower the price, the greater the sales

An economic rule is that when a price is lowered for a particular product, the quantity of that product demanded, that is, the number of items sold from your catalog, rises. The prospect likes to hear the term *sale,* 30 percent off, just reduced, reduced for a limited time, and act today for reduced price. When your price is lower, it enables the value to exceed the price more easily, and the prospect is more apt to respond with the necessary action to buy. I recommend you keep your lead product low enough in the beginning stages of your business to sell the maximum orders. By selling maximum orders of a lead product, for example a special software package, you will be able to develop a rapport with the customer and build up your house mailing list. Your house mailing list is your customers who bought from your catalog. Certain products kept at a low-end price will give the potential long-term customer a chance to see, use, and tell others about your product. Word-of-mouth advertisements are the least expensive and most powerful way to promote your products and catalog. Statistics show that when your customer is satisfied with your product or service, she or he will tell 10 others. This is another reason to ask your customer to give you the names and addresses of friends and associates at work who would like to receive your next catalog.

Pricing is based on your business philosophy

As a general rule many catalog and mail order operators want to get 3 to 4 times cost, or at minimum 2 to 3 times cost. For example, in full-cost pricing, if your product had a cost to you by the manufacturer of $15, to get 3 times cost you would have to price it at $45 ($3 \times 15$). For the higher-priced product, $60 or more, you might want to reduce your markup. A general rule is that the lower the cost of the product, the higher the markup. For example, a product with a $2 cost must sell for $6 to $8 for you to earn a reliable profit. Review the following situation.

Product	Cost to you	Price at 2 × cost	Price at 3 × cost	Price at 4 × cost	Total sales of 1000
A	$20	$40			$40,000
A	20		$60		60,000
A	20			$80	80,000

Trying to get the maximum price for your product or service is tempting, but sales are easier to make when potential customers feel they are getting the best possible price for the product or service they intend to buy. Catalog selling is a difficult business, and your price must be well planned and matched to the product being offered. Will the prospect get the best possible product for the price? If not, will the customer order again and use the product regularly and tell others about your business and products? Your price is an important strategy which can help you compete and succeed in this business.

Test your pricing

Pricing can be tested to determine which price will work hard to sell the most products for you. You can do the price testing in your space advertisements or in your catalog itself. For example, if you are selling product AA, and you want to test the prices, $22.95 and $25.99, run it in two different issues of a magazine such as *Popular Mechanics,* or *The Wall Street Journal,* and check the sales results. Look at the results below:

Date	Publication	Type	Price	Sales	Total
9/97	*Popular Mechanics*	Display	$22.95	150	$3,442.50
11/97	*Popular Mechanics*	Display	25.99	132	3,430.68
Difference					$ 11.82

Your $22.95 price beat the $25.99 price by $11.82, and if you used the lower price in the 11/97 advertisement, you would earn an additional profit for future sales. Once you find a price which works, keep using it until the sales start to drop.

Review your cost before you set a price

Too often new catalog marketing owners get so excited and enthusiastic about the business, they stop thinking about their costs and look directly at the price times their total possible sales, losing all grip on reality. Your costs are real. No one is selling you merchandise, shipping services, postage, envelopes, packages, writing and creative services for free, all these are going to be charged to you, and staying in business will require that you pass these expenses along to your customers. Let's take a look at the profit for product A and determine the real profit in this sale. Once we get the net profit per product, we can then determine the breakeven point—the amount of orders you will need to pay for all your costs and from which point you will be earning a profit.

Product A

Full-Cost Analysis

Sales	
Price per product A	$15.00
Adjusted price of product	3.00
Total price	$18.00

Costs	
Purchasing and unit cost of product A	5.00
Adm. expenses for handling, order processing	0.95
Packaging (boxes, tape, etc.)	0.50
Shipping (UPS or postage)	1.60
Sales taxes	0.90
Handling returns	0.55
Credit card processing	0.50
Administrative overhead	1.50
Printing catalogs, postage	0.50
Total costs	12.00
Net profit (sales = costs)	$6.00

Notice that the purchasing and administrative costs are very high; if these important charges were not included in your price, you would not get the profit margin you need to succeed in your business. Purchasing and administrative costs will vary with volume of your business. Now remember, this is not a lead product, and you want to sell, but you want to get your profit so you can buy new products, mail catalogs, and keep selling. You will earn $6.00 profit on the product list above. Use this format to establish your own profit projection.

Base your selling price on the amount of products you expect to sell during the next year. For illustrative purposes, you will find a formula to determine your selling price for your product. I would like you to use this formula for all your products, so you will realize just what profit you can expect. You will use the following formula to arrive at your selling price for the product A we discussed in the cost analysis just presented:

$$SP = \frac{(C \times US) + P + O}{US}$$

where SP = the selling price for the product

C = the unit cost of the product

US = the anticipated unit sales of the product for the period

P = the anticipated profit for the period
O = the overhead and related purchasing costs

Now, using the previous full-cost analysis, let's determine the selling price for product A, assuming you expect to sell at least 1000 products. We solved the equation in the following manner.

$$SP = \frac{(\$5 \times 1000) + 6000 + 7000}{1000}$$ (See full-cost analysis on previous page.)

$$SP = \frac{\$5000 + 6000 + 7000}{1000}$$

$$SP = \frac{\$18,000}{1000}$$

$$SP = \$18$$

Use the breakeven analysis

Since we just determined that you would use $18 for the selling price, this is based on you selling 1000 units of product A. However, you're not sure this will happen—at best, this is your estimate—so you need to know what will happen when you sell more or less than this number. To determine this you will need the following formula:

$$BEP = \frac{\text{Cost (product) overhead}}{\text{Selling price}}$$

Using the number from the previous example, you will determine the breakeven point in the following manner:

$$BEP = \frac{12,000}{18}$$

$$= 667$$

So you will need 667 orders to break even; you cannot earn a profit until you reach this point. To succeed, don't be satisfied with just breaking even, set goals and attain sales to earn the best profits possible. Evaluate each product or service for profitability and change losers for a winner.

Summary

Pricing is another important strategy to give your consumers a reason to buy from you. People watch prices closely but look at value versus the price. Lead products must be priced low enough to do the job. Keep up with your competitors' products. Review the possible demand for your product. Look at various price ideas before you finalize your decision. Test your price. Review all your costs, not just some of them. Do a full-cost analysis. Check the breakeven analysis. Now let's discuss writing the copy for your catalog.

7

Writing your catalog successfully

I recall one of my seminar attendees who, during a discussion on writing effective copy to get the best possible sales results, turned to me and said, "This is easy, I would hire the best possible copy writer and let the writer do it." This is an option, but I suggest you attempt the writing of your catalog copy yourself to get the experience; this experience will pay off when you decide you want to hire someone else to write copy, because you will possess knowledge to evaluate it correctly. By the time you are ready to write, you should know more about your product or service than anyone else. Why not do the writing yourself? You are the expert. You can do it, just try. Let's discuss the process of writing successful catalog copy.

A good copy writer knows the facts and benefits about the product or service

The copy writer for a catalog on antique reproductions must know as many facts about the reproduction as possible. Place the product in the room in which you are writing, put it on your desk, look at it in an interesting way, focus on the ways it will benefit the people who will buy it. Talk to people who own and use the product. What do they say about it? Get any positive testimonials, and once you get their permission to use a testimonial, include it in your catalog copy.

Use testimonials of satisfied customers

You will add to your copy by telling your prospects what other people enjoyed about your product, how the product satisfied them enough to buy it again. You can get testimonials from customers who write to you, or some catalog owners get them from customers by just asking for them. The key is to get their permission before you use their names. A testimonial is listed below.

> I am very happy with the golf clubs I purchased from you last spring. When I returned one club broken in transit, you sent me another without charge. Keep up the good work.
>
> CHARLES SMITHLY
> *Hawthorne, NY*

Here is the consent letter you should have your customer sign before you use their testimonials:

> I, Charles Smithly, agree to permit ABC Catalog Company to use my letter of January 7, 1997, for a testimonial in future catalogs.
>
> CHARLES SMITHLY

The competition in the catalog business is very intense, and many of your prospects will only read your catalog if your words and initial presentation appeal to them enough to continue the reading. Many catalogs are thrown in the waste baskets or put away, never to be opened again. To avoid this fate, you must be willing to do the necessary research on your product or service to present it in an interesting, fast moving manner. Get to know your company's strategy and review the reasons that you selected this product in the first place. Use the product yourself. It will be easier to sell a fax machine in your catalog when you use and run a fax machine each day at your office. Tell the prospect how you save time; deal directly with your customers using the facts how the fax sends a copy immediately to a company a country away. Go ahead and tell them how the fax can benefit them. Define the product or service fully. Get all the definitions of your product from the dictionaries, articles about it, or how it is presently being used. Know the history of the product. When was it developed? Who developed it? How was it sold and distributed? Is it sold in other catalogs? Tell customers if you're the only dealer for it. What are the uses of the product? Who uses it? Small businesses? Hospitals? Large businesses? Attorneys? Accountants? Consultants?

Write to your market. Write directly to the customer just like you are writing a personal letter. Review any other advertisements or publicity used to sell the product or service in the past. This would include small-space advertisements; large-space advertisements; and news releases, which are publicity sent to magazines and newspapers to introduce a product or to educate the public when a product is being improved. You can get much of this information from your dealer or manufacturer. Get to know the product or service that has been presented to the public or to a target market. Gather as much information as possible before you write the first word in your catalog copy. Have more information than you need, and then choose only the most powerful and moving copy possible. Make it interesting. Below you will find a checklist.

Before-You-Start-Writing Checklist

1. List the reasons that your product or service can help your prospect. ____
2. Develop a good lead sentence using benefits such as "save money." ____
3. Know your prospect and your product thoroughly. ____
4. Bring the prospect and product together with clear writing. ____
5. Use a friendly, businesslike approach. ____
6. Ask for the order, tell the prospect how to order right away. ____
7. Sell the prospect, and keep selling over and over. ____

Visualize and understand your market

Who is your prospect? Where does he or she live? How much money does she or he earn? What are his or her goals in life? Successful copy writers take the time to learn their prospects completely so when they write the copy it appeals to them directly. For example, I know a catalog marketing owner who sells to convenience store owners all over the United States. When we discussed this market, I asked my friend to think about the life of a convenience store owner who juggles endless duties, from ordering an attractive line of goods, hiring and scheduling help, training the help, paying for the goods, sorting, grading, and pricing the goods to try to give the best customer service possible. This might be one of the most difficult market segments to sell to today, and in order to sell this group you need lively, friendly, and benefit-oriented copy. The average or below-average copy will die, fall flat on its face. The convenience store owners get plenty of mail from catalog owners and manufacturers who want to sell to them. Tell the convenience store owner how your product will sell and make money for him or her right away. Inform the owner how your product will produce hundreds of dollars per week if he or she will give you some valuable shelf space to offer your product to the customers of the store.

How do you really get to know your market?

In a few words: you go out and find out what makes your customer tick. Stop in your local convenience store and during a slow time mid-afternoon or mid-morning and talk with the owner. You might even consider taking a part-time job in the store to get added exposure to the business. Ask questions and observe what is going on in that store from morning to night, seven days a week. Nothing takes the place of getting closer to your target market. Once you understand customers, you can then write copy which meets their needs.

You can test your copy

Writing successful copy takes practice, understanding, and the ability to change your copy when it fails. For example, you mail out 1000 catalogs selling personal care products to convenience store owners, and your copy stresses the basic guarantee of your product and the quality of your reputation in the field. On the order form in your catalog you will key this copy approach with the letter *Q*. The address on your order card will look like the following:

ABC Catalog Sales
10 Main St., Suite 100Q
Anytown, USA 00001

Another mailing of 1000 catalogs with a different approach such as a focus on making money—"your stock will turn over faster, increasing your profits"—uses the key *M*. The address on your order card will say:

ABC Catalog Sales
10 Main St., Suite 100M
Anytown, USA 00001

It will be very easy to test which copy is working. Did the copy approach on quality keyed with *Q* get more orders than copy approach for earning money keyed with the *M?* It is not necessarily the amount of orders which really counts; the total dollars are essential. Review the following:

Copy Approach Test

Date	Copy key	Orders	Percentage	Total sales
Jan. 1997	*Q*	10	1.000	$250.00
Jan. 1997	*A*	8	0.075	375.00

Your job as a copywriter is to sell, sell for as many dollars as possible. Use the copy approach which will work for you. In order to succeed in the catalog business, you must get readers to read, then convince them to buy. A tried and tested method is the AIDA sales process of writing copy. AIDA stands for attention, interest, desire, and action. Successful copy follows this process.

Attention is gained by a good headline or striking photograph of the product or service. Some catalog owners keep a product or photograph next to them as they write copy. Give your target market what it needs to know to buy from you. Stop customers in their tracks. A catalog marketer created interest by discussing a leather military jacket, told the prospect it was a genuine military issue, not a reproduction, that it was made in the United States, capturing the patriotic sentiments from World War II to Somalia. Desire was cultivated by describing the knitted cuffs and waistband, military snap-down collar, and the full guarantee. Some writers of catalog copy call this selling the sizzle rather than the steak. Discuss just enough to create desire to sell your product. Now you have set your catalog reader up for the action stage to check the item off with a pencil or pen and then list it on the order form. To get this important action is asking for the order. Tell the reader it is offered in blue, brown, and grey, and, if action is taken by February 10th, a special 10 percent is taken off the regular price of $199.00—so the coat can be purchased for $179.10.

Choose a theme which relates to your market

You know that your market, your strategy, and your products create a theme which ties them all together. For example, a catalog marketer selling automotive products to help save gasoline decided on a theme, "Save Money and Energy." Another marketer, selling electronic products and toys, uses the theme, "Products Which Think." Work on a theme which will give you an opportunity to sell more products. A marketer of medical supplies sold to physicians has a theme offering free products when certain products are purchased. This theme failed, because doctors are not supposed to accept inducements under their strict code of ethics. Once you develop a theme which you feel will work, go with it. Carefully check your results. To succeed in the writing copy game, you must be willing to test, then make the changes, and then test and change until you get the successful theme. Once you get results, leave it alone. Ride the success train.

Use the power words to get the order

Some words motivate people to act. The power words connect to the reader; they help the prospects visualize how the product or service will benefit or help them in their lives. Your copy should be *you* oriented. *You* is the most important power word. *You* will succeed using our product. *You* will earn extra money. *You* will meet new people. *You* will be the life of the party. *You* will learn a career. *You* will drive the best car in town. *You* will play better golf. *You* will look more attractive. Everyone wants products which can help them personally. Below you will find *power words* to add to your catalog copy:

You	Special	Save	Attractive
Discover	Innovation	Proven	Family
Guarantee	Security	Today	Winning
Gain	Ensure	Victory	Financial gain

These power words are not complicated words; they are simple, yet they are words which hook people to read more and to act to order the product. These power words build up your case, just as a lawyer builds a case before going to trial. The power words build your case so your customer will consider your offer more fully and order from you. Use power words and sell.

Another secret to writing successful copy is to include the offer in your copy. The offer is the elements you proposition to your prospect, and the offer will include your product, price, terms, incentives, and guarantees. Too often many copy writers forget that each prospect reviews the offer before making a decision. Note the offer for the product below.

The Offer

Product	Money clip
Price	$14.99
Terms	Cash, credit card
Incentive	10 percent discount
Guarantee	Full guarantee

As an example of copy writing, assume that your product is a handcrafted bookcase called the "Fireside Reading Bench"; it offers storage to accommodate 30 to 35 books. Your research shows the dimensions and weight are 42"L × 16 3/4"H × 11 1/2"D and approximately 28 lbs. The wood is a solid red oak, and it is finished in classic, antique, or Jamestown. After fully examining the bench, you determine that this bookcase has two basic benefits: it holds the books, and you can sit on the bench while reading, saving space in your home for other furniture. Let's look at one approach you can use to sell this product in your next catalog:

> Exciting, new Shaker-style bookcase for the book lovers in your family. It can hold over 30 books and serves as a handsome bench for relaxing while reading by the fireplace, in the den, family room, or living room. It will serve as an excellent birthday, anniversary, wedding gift. Purchase by October 15th, and save an extra $10—regular price is $179, yours now for only $169. Act now, while supplies last. Fully guaranteed.

Notice how this copy uses the power words such as *guaranteed* and *new* and shows the benefits of using the bookcase as a reading bench. This copy gives the many possible uses in the home, how the product can be located in various rooms or locations in the home, and how it can be used as a gift item or for many other occasions.

Copy must pay the rent

Your catalog might have 50 to 75 products or services once you get started fully, and each product and copy must pull its weight to pay for the amount of space it uses in the catalog. For example, let's say your catalog is on home-based business books, and you used one full page of your catalog to feature one of your new books—*Home-Based Newsletter Publishing*—and the size of the catalog is 20 pages. Then one full page space in a 20-page catalog is 1/20 of the catalog or 5 percent of the total cost of putting a catalog together and mailing it out. The copy and the product must be evaluated, such as the presentation below:

Product	Catalog pages	Space used	Percent of catalog	Catalog preparation, printing, mailing costs per 1000	Sales required for product A, based on 5%	Actual sales for product A	Profit or loss on product A per 1000	Remarks
A	20	1 full page	5	$1,210.00	$60.50 (1,210 x 5%)	$105.00	$44.50 profit	Continue

Notice how in the case of product A the sales were $105, and they needed to beat the 5 percent rental and cost charges of $60.50; the product did so and made a profit of $44.50, therefore the page can stay in the catalog for a longer period of time. Every product must pull sales or will be replaced, but to give each product or service a chance to make it requires the best possible copy to tell the best story to the target market. The copy is the salesperson making a presentation to the potential customer and must work for you. Evaluate your sales performance for each product and copy regularly, and just as a landlord must turn a nonpaying tenant out to find a new apartment you must find new products and copy to replace the nonperforming products in your catalog.

Don't imitate another catalog's copy style

Avoid the temptation to use the same method of copy writing as a successful competitor. Do it your way. Carve out your own communication method to reach your potential customer in a manner which meets your personality and understanding of the field and treats the potential buyer professionally. Be willing to swim upstream and do things completely differently, and this will set you apart from the rest of the pack. You are a special person, and your products or services are chosen especially for this target market; therefore design your copy approach and put it to work.

Summary

Getting the best copy for your catalog is more than simply hiring a copywriter to do it for you. You are the expert on your products and services; use this knowledge. Know all the facts about and benefits of your products. Good copy writing alone may not beat the competition; it must be the best possible copy writing to get the orders. Present your product in an interesting, entertaining, and fast-moving way. Use the product or service yourself before you write about it. Use testimonials. Visualize and get to know your target market. Focus on your offer. Call potential customers to get to know them better. Visit potential customers at their places of business to get a feel for their problems, concerns, pressures, and lifestyles. Test your copy to see which approach is working. Key your copy approach. Use the AIDA approach. Focus on a theme which relates to your market and use power words to help you hook the customer. Showcase the little-known benefits of your product. Your copy must pay the rent to stay in your catalog—each product or service must make a profit to stay in the catalog for the next issue.

8

Designing and producing your catalog

This is the challenge you have earned by doing your homework, to choose the product, select the strategy, and choose the best possible market. Now you want to make your catalog look so impressive that your prospects will read it, spend some of their valuable time with it, think about your offer, and then take action by ordering from you.

Make your catalog cover jump out and grab the readers attention, cultivate interest and desire, and score the most important point in the business: Get the order. A sample cover is shown in Fig. 8-1. Designing your catalog means looking at the competition and reviewing how other catalogs present their products or services, but this is just the beginning of the process and not the end. Be creative. Be different. Look at your product or service in a different way. Tip it upside down, turn it sideways, look at the product from the sky. Permit your product or service to grow to the maximum by showing all the important benefits, uses, ideas, and appeals possible. Use every strategy within your arsenal to show your product in the best possible light.

Figure 8-1. Catalog cover. Get attention to your catalog by offering a catalog cover that appeals directly to your readers and future customers.

A case history

A 7-million-dollar-a-year catalog marketing owner in Ukiah, California, John Schaeffer has developed a unique catalog catering to the energy field called *Real Goods.* Instead of the usual product listing method, he uses a community magazine format, including letters on political articles, commentary, and passionate letters on the energy movement. Schaeffer found that once he started to establish a rapport with his readers and forced them to think, the problem of how to get orders took care of itself. Schaeffer gets many ideas from his customers; at last count, 10 percent of all catalog selections are customer inspired, and many customers tell him what products should be manufactured by the company. The real payoff for a well-designed catalog is the rapport you develop with your customers. Once the customers accept your catalog as being part of their inner circle or family, they will buy and continue to buy from you.

Become a catalog junkie

One direct marketing expert claimed she became an expert by reading and searching magazines and catalogs for photographs and art techniques which present the product or service in an appealing way. Remember that your main goal is to present your product in a way which shows all the benefits, features, uses, and appeals to your specific reader. Keep a folder of visual ideas you find in other catalogs or mailing pieces.

Good graphics means setting an image

Good graphics means following along with the theme or personality you want to establish with your prospect. For example when the theme is choosing gifts for the Christmas holiday season, you want to connect to your prospect with many Christmas and New Year settings. When your theme is selling business information to compete with the global business competition, show your product or service in situations so the reader gets the specific information needed to become a winner. Blend your artwork into the image you want to deliver to be successful.

Format and size

The format and the size of your catalog are important considerations because they will affect the visual look of your catalog and can affect the price you will pay for the printing of your catalog. The most common sizes are $8\frac{1}{2} \times 11$", $5\frac{1}{2} \times 8\frac{1}{2}$", and 8×9". Choose the one which you feel will work for you. See examples of catalog sizes in the figure on page 72. The format is the way your visuals and copy will be presented on each page of your catalog. For example, some catalog owners use a format where products are presented in blocks, including both visual and copy, throughout the pages of the catalog. Still other catalog owners want to fully display the product, so they use a much larger percentage of the page for visuals and a small amount for copy. The figure shows examples of both formats.

Review other catalogs to determine which ones give the best visual look for your products or services. Research shows that people read from the left to the right and need lots of information about features, benefits, and reasons that they should buy your product before they'll buy. You want to mail a catalog with the best format and designed with the proper setting, so your catalog can get the order.

Sizes

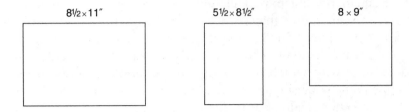

Formats

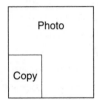

Copy and artwork are teammates

The words you use are important because your copy presents a case to your reader much like an attorney presents a case to the jury in the courtroom. In catalog selling, just like in the courtroom, decisions can be made more easily when information such as photographs, artwork, drawings, and graphs are used to fully educate and inform the reader. An important question in many of my seminars is: What comes first, words or pictures? The answer is simple: The words. Put the words out first and then review visual ideas. Determine whether you want to use a drawing, a photograph which sells the product, a graph, or a chart. Tie the copy together with the best picture. When you use a photograph of a person other than a family member, you must get a model's release, which is a person's permission to use their photograph in your catalog. A simple model's release is given below:

> I, Reginald Van Cloud, on this day of January 5, 1998, hereby offer permission to Johnson's Safety Products Catalog Company to use my photograph, modeling the X401 safety glasses.
>
> SINCERELY,
> REGINALD VAN CLOUD

Get the model release signed before you use the photograph; one large advertising agency tried to use a photograph without a release and was sued.

Where can you get your artwork?

You can draw yourself, photograph yourself, hire an artist or photographer, or buy stock artwork. Some people use a book of clip artwork—see one example in Fig. 8-2—or art on a computer disk, which allows you to have free use of all the art. You can purchase stock photographs at photograph companies which specialize in this business. Many mail order catalog owners use stock photographs rather than hire a professional photographer to do a photo setting. The stock photograph company will charge you according to the way you use the photograph. Are you sending out 5000, 10,000, 100,000 catalogs, or using the photograph in a magazine display advertisement in a national news magazine? You want to use the artwork which will appeal and attract your prospect visually.

Sometimes the use of line drawings along with photographs on the same catalog page can be striking and gain attention and

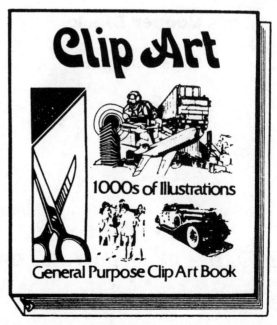

Figure 8-2. Clip art book. The clip art book is an excellent way to add artwork and illustrations to your catalog at a low cost.

readership. People born after the year 1955 are more apt to read attentively when photographs and artwork are used.

Show the product in action

One catalog owner selling portable calculators shows how the product can be held easily in hand, used at the desk or bench, used next to the phone at home, or by a salesperson in a car or riding in a plane. Your artwork opens the door to benefits, uses, and appeals which will help you sell more products. The catalog marketer selling leisure wear clothing can show how readers can look more attractive golfing, dining out, touring a major attraction, going to a ball game, or shopping at a mall.

Typography is an art form

Blend your photograph ad copy together with the correct typography, a special process setting and arranging typefaces, and then present them in printed form. There are many typefaces. Below you will find some sample typefaces just to give you some ideas. These are samples of FaceLift Fonts:

Dutch Bold

Cooper Black

Swiss Bold Italic

Brush Script

Formal Script

Park Ave

Be careful in choosing typefaces if you plan on using text set in all capital letters. Some type styles are not suitable for all caps:

THIS IS PARK AVE IN ALL CAPS

THIS IS BRUSH SCRIPT IN CAPS

Typefaces are either serif, which is characterized by having "feet" at the edges of each letter, or sans serif, which is plain (see Fig.

**This is a sample of
a Sans Serif type
without feet.**

This is a sample of
a Serif type
notice the little
feet.

Figure 8-3. Choose the sans serif or the serif type for your catalog typography. Once a decision is made, continue with the same typography.

8-3). Some catalog owners tested prospects with both typefaces and found the serif type was read faster than the sans serif. Review both typefaces before you make a decision. Once you choose a typeface, continue to use it catalog after catalog. Constant changing from one typeface to another will confuse your reader, and you lose the consistency with your reader as well.

Choose the type alignment for your catalog

The type alignment is another consideration in your catalog design. The example below is flush left type, ragged right, which simply means that only the first letter in each line of type is aligned. This example is taken from a catalog on books:

#109
SECRETS TO SUCCESS IN YOUR JOB
Success. Everyone is trying to make a success at work, especially today with the difficult and competitive conditions in today's workplace.

Whether you feel your career is at a plateau, or if you believe things are going well, but could be even better, I'm certain your plans for the future get new thrust from the newly revised book, *"Secrets to Success in Your Job."*

Another possible alignment for your catalog is the justified type, in which the type is set so that both margins align. See the example below, selling a product, which uses the justified alignment:

> belt driven equipment. Adjusts from 4⅜" to 15⅜" with supplied spacer tubes. Ruggedly made of chrome plated brass and steel.
>   **V-6389** Belt tensioner **$14.25**

Each page is a masterpiece

Each page of your catalog is a salesperson for you, presenting your product or service and asking for the order. Getting the order in today's competitive marketplace will require that each product is carefully presented in the best possible light with catalog copy which is descriptive and marketing oriented. Don't fall into the trap of playing favorites whereby you give special attention to some products and the others get the once over. Every product or service is a star, and you must present it well. Put together products which tell a story for that page, make the page an enjoyable read, like a novelist does for readers. Successful catalogs are done one page at a time.

Lay out each page

A layout is a specific plan for where you want to place each product on the page, and just how the text or typography will blend into the page. Your layout will move from a very rough layout to a more definitive layout as shown in Fig. 8-4.

What are the advantages of using typography?

There are many advantages for you. Typography being set saves space. You save money in your printing, it is more attractive, easier on the reader's eye, can be read faster, and can set your product or service apart from your competition. There are many software packages available to give you a variety of typefaces; find one to meet your needs. Remember, do not copy a competitor's typeface; develop your own design identity.

Logo is your signature to your reader

Your logo is your graphic image, and the goal is to give your readers some insight into your line of products and a way to remember you. Some catalog owners use the title of their catalog as their logo,

Figure 8-4. Layout of page. Plan how each page will present your product and services. You can move from a rough layout to a detailed layout.

and they use this in all catalogs, on their sales letters, envelopes, and shipping boxes. Use the logo to get maximum results from it. Try to choose a logo which can be reproduced easily.

Your design and preparation can be done for you

I know how you're feeling right now—there are so many considerations in the design and preparing of your catalog, especially if you have had little experience in printing. You're in luck; a number of printers specialize in taking your catalog from the layout, photography, composition (typography), and finally to the printing. This can be a decision you might want to make if you feel you lack the time to do the work yourself. Never expect printers to handle the design unless they specialize in this area, such as a catalog specialist printer. Review their previous work completely. Get quotations from as many printers as possible before you make a decision. Consider quality and price.

Another option is to talk with a graphic artist who is experienced in catalog preparation and ask him or her about handling the design and layout for your catalog. A catalog owner in Louisiana asked a graphic artist to consult with him for an hour—and paid for the consulting time. The consulting meeting helped the owner to decide on the best graphic and design elements for his catalog. You may decide this is an option for you. One final idea on design of your catalog: Start small with your catalog, do a smaller catalog in the beginning, say, 8 to 10 pages, and by doing your first mailing this will be a test on your design. Evaluate your results and then make the necessary changes as you go along. It is more important to start the catalog and then do the testing, than to spend too much time trying to get the masterpiece and never sending it out.

Summary

Become a catalog junkie. Your graphic design gives you an image—choose the best format and size. Art work and copy are teammates; there are many ways to obtain art work. Products in action sell better. Your typography is an art form. There are many advantages to using typography. Choose a proper type alignment for your catalog. Each page should be laid out to become a masterpiece. Your logo is your signature. Get help if you need it for your catalog by choosing a specialist printer or a graphic artist.

9

Preparing your catalog for printing

You are now ready to join your copy and graphics elements to make the very best impression on your readers possible. Research shows that getting the readers' attention in the beginning of the process will help you sell more products. Place your new, exciting, appealing products in the beginning of your catalog. A catalog owner from Delaware places his lead products in the first few pages of the catalog and runs a careful check of the sales for each product; the winners stay in the catalog, the losers are screened out.

Preparation starts with a page layout

Let's say you decide to do a 10-page catalog on books. How do you get your layout on your page so you can get the best presentation of your products or services? Start with a rough layout for page 2 of your catalog as shown in Fig. 9-1. Be willing to prepare numerous layouts until you get it just the way you want it. Strive for the best layout possible, and then go on to the next step, which is placing the typography on the printed page. This is also called a mechanical stage, because you are placing the elements together to prepare for printing mechanically (see Fig. 9-2). Remember, in the mechanical you might not get all the

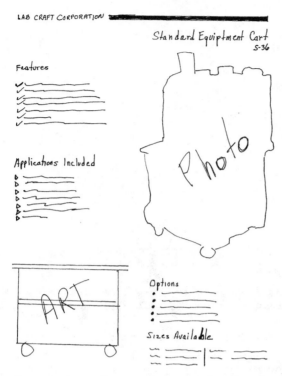

Figure 9-1. Preparation of printed material. After the layout, prepare a mechanical (artwork and typography) and bring the original artwork and photographs to the printer.

products or services and copy on one page, but you have more than one page, so simply move them to the next page. The mechanical will be taken to the printer to use for the printing process. Place a tissue sheet over the mechanical to prevent it from getting soiled or damaged while in your possession or at the printers. The mechanical is the final process before the printing, so look it over carefully. The mechanical represents to the photocopy machine, platemaker, or process camera exactly how your catalog will look. In short, your mechanical must be reviewed completely, not just from a technical point of view; it has instructions for the printer, but from a reader's point of view, it sends a clear message to the readers and makes such an impression that it sells your product and services. One catalog owner from Florida puts his full name and address on each mechanical and checks the artwork for each one; he then checks the typography on all mechanicals to make sure it is secure; he

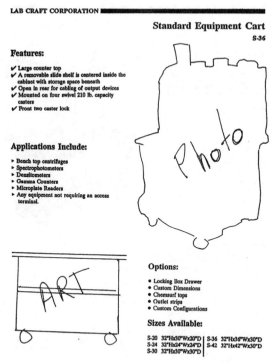

LAB CRAFT CORPORATION

Standard Equipment Cart
S-36

Features:

✔ Large counter top
✔ A removable slide shelf is centered inside the cabinet with storage space beneath
✔ Open in rear for cabling of output devices
✔ Mounted on four swivel 210 lb. capacity casters
✔ Front two caster lock

Applications Include:

▸ Bench top centrifuges
▸ Spectrophotometers
▸ Densitometers
▸ Gamma Counters
▸ Microplate Readers
▸ Any equipment not requiring an access terminal.

Options:

● Locking Box Drawer
● Custom Dimensions
● Chemsurf tops
● Outlet strips
● Custom Configurations

Sizes Available:

S-20	32"Hx30"Wx20"D	S-36	32"Hx36"Wx30"D
S-24	32"Hx24"Wx24"D	S-42	32"Hx42"Wx30"D
S-30	32"Hx30"Wx30"D		

Figure 9-2. Your mechanical offers the finished typography and shows the placement for photographs and artwork.

then makes photocopies of each mechanical which stay in his possession after the mechanicals go to the printer.

The last step in the process is to take the mounted photography or artwork you plan to use for page 2 and take it to the printer. Now you have everything you need to print up the printed catalog page. Notice, I am talking about only one page. I want you to consider only one page at a time. Each page is important as a unit, and together the pages will be turned into successful printing pieces. The finished page is shown in Fig. 9-3.

Try to keep your catalog as easy to produce as possible

Many successful catalog owners develop a quality catalog, mail it out on time, and give excellent service. The key element to their success is that they keep their catalog to a reasonable size, make it easy to assemble, and deliver what their readers need to order.

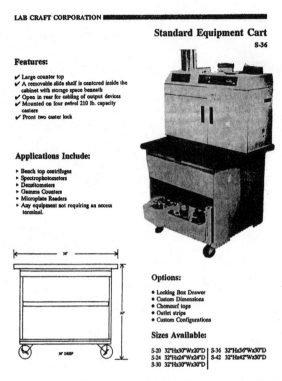

Figure 9-3. The printed page includes all the typography, artwork, and photographs to sell to your customers.

For example, a catalog sent to purchasing agents to purchase parts may need little artwork but must have the part numbers and terms to give the readers what they need. Some catalogs lend themselves to artwork and photographs while others do not. You can make the determination of which strategy you would like to use.

Do a dummy catalog before you print it

Too often beginner catalog marketing owners print up their catalog too soon and print many thousands of catalogs before determining that many other options could have made it a better catalog. Review the dummy catalog along with other people whose opinions you value and trust. You can make the dummy catalog by putting the typography and artwork together along with the order card. Make the dummy look as close to the printed catalog as possible. Mail it to 5 or 10 people with a note or letter enclosed that you would like them to examine the catalog and fill out the order card for the products or services they felt they would order from you. Send a catalog to yourself at your home or office. Examine it yourself and grade the catalog in the following areas:

Yes   *No*

1. Does the cover appeal to you?

2. Did you enjoy reading and reviewing the complete catalog?

3. Did you find a good selection of products and/or services?

4. What product or service stood out from the others?

_____

5. How many products or services would you purchase?

_____

6. Did you find any misspellings, incorrect words in the copy?

_____

7. Please name any products or services you would purchase.

_____

8. What general impressions do you get from the catalog?

_____

_____

Gather up the information from the other people; if they fail to send it back to you, call them by phone, ask them the questions, and carefully fill out all the answers. People's honest reactions are essential to you. This is the last test before you print the catalog and mail it out to your market. Review all the responses and check to see if there are any patterns to the criticisms—can anything be corrected? Did any of your readers agree with your own evaluation? Review the dummy catalog and make the necessary corrections.

Summary

Your layout is essential to a professional catalog. Move from the layout to placing your typography and art placement on the mechanical artwork. The mechanical and the mounted photography or drawings will be taken to the printer. Your mechanical is essential to the quality printing job. Keep it clean and protected from damage and always keep an extra copy—sometimes printers lose mechanicals. As a test, prepare a dummy catalog and send it out to 5 to 10 people who will be honest enough to give you a frank opinion of your catalog. Look over the evaluations fully.

10

Printing your catalog

You have now prepared your mechanical artwork and are ready to get the complete catalog printed. Printing is not some mysterious process, but one which is possible to learn, and one which can be mastered. One of the first steps in getting the best possible printing work is to know what you want for printing specifications. For example, do you want two-color, which is black and another color, or four-color printing, which is blue, red, yellow, and black? Do you want a four-color cover and your pages printed in basic black-and-white printing? What type of paper stock do you want to use? Some catalog owners use photographs and drawings together. How many photographs are you going to use in your catalog? How many line drawings are you going to use? Review the printing specifications sheet below:

	Black and white	Two-color	Four-color
Cover			
Order form			
Pages			
Back cover			

Too often new catalog marketing owners just assume that they will choose the four-color printing for all pages of their catalog without giving enough thought to at least testing the various printing alternatives and letting the catalog readers decide whether the color of the printing affects their purchasing decision. For example you can send out 1000 copies of your catalog with a two-color cover and all pages in black and white; then for the second group print 1000 copies with four-color printing from cover to all the complete pages. Some products and services lend themselves to black-and-white printing, whereas others really need color printing to boost the sales.

Review the organization of your catalog

A catalog owner selling industrial products reviews his catalog for three special points before turning it over to the printer: (1) he makes certain the reader gets the production information necessary to buy, (2) he makes certain his visual presentation fits the image he wants to convey, and (3) he uses a guide such as a table of contents to assign different product classifications to keep the reader moving along in his catalog. Once you get a catalog with the best possible organization, you can then take it to your printer.

Choose the printer carefully

Choose the very best printer to offer you the quality for the money you decide to spend. Avoid the mistake of the catalog owner from New Hampshire, who was told by a friend to hire a printer, and when the owner turned the work over to this unknown printer who was not evaluated, the results were poor. The catalog had poor printing quality, smudges, and the costs were much more than if a first-class printer had been hired originally. There are many different printers, from quick printers, which specialize in short-run work, to specialty printers who specialize in brochures, newsletters, stationery, wedding invitations, and invoices; catalog printers specialize in printing catalog sheets and catalogs. Catalog sheets are separate sheets of specific pages of your catalog which you can send to specific customers, or, if you have a sales team, they can use these sheets in their sales presentations. Many of these printers are listed in your local or regional city telephone book. You can choose the best printer by visiting some printers in your neighborhood. Ask to see some of their work, especially their catalogs or catalog sheets. Take this a step further and call the customers who had their catalogs printed and ask whether they were satisfied with the XYZ Printer

Company, in Greyville, Illinois. Did they meet your deadline? Would you do business with them again? If not, why not? If yes, why yes? Be willing to listen to the former customers about what they learned from their printing experiences. Make some notes to be used later in your final printing vendor selection decision.

Schedule your printing accordingly

Too often catalog owner and printer get into problems because of a too tight printing schedule; both parties get irritated, and all parties lose out. The catalog owner wants the catalog next week, the printer really wants to do the work, accepts the difficult time schedule, and, once the work begins, realizes that this tight deadline cannot be met. To avoid this, give yourself and your printer sufficient time to complete the work so that the work and the quality will be the highest level possible. Rushing the work can cause mistakes, and these mistakes cost money. Below you will find a printing schedule for a children's catalog for an owner in Vermont.

Scheduling for Catalog Printing

Date camera-ready artwork delivered to printer	January 15, 1999
Date of completion	January 30, 1999

The catalog owner does not need the catalogs until the tentative mailing date of February 8, 1999, so the full nine days between picking up the printing work until the mailing date gives some extra time just in case of final corrections, or a press breaking down, or some slowdown at the printer. Give yourself enough time; the printer will be happy you built in this extra time.

Do one printing job at a time. Focus on your catalog exclusively during the printing process. Print up your business cards, stationery, envelopes, or other printing needs at a different time. This gives the printer the opportunity to focus on the main objective, your catalog. Permit the printer to do the best work possible.

Tell your printer of your plans and your needs

Just as your artwork and copy tries to focus on your customer, you should take the time to discuss with your printer your goals for your catalog, what type of customer you are trying to serve, and what products and services are being targeted to your customer. Let the printer know you plan to print catalogs on a regular basis, and when he or she shows you top quality and price, he or she could get the steady work from you.

Review the paper stock available

In the catalog business, the paper is your stock and trade, and you want to choose the best grade of paper which can present your products or services. Some catalog owners use the coated stock, and others use the plain bond paper. Get the printer to show you what she or he recommends for paper and take a sample sheet with you. Put the sheet of sample paper in your copy machine, make a copy of one of your mechanicals, for say, page 3, and you will get a chance to see, feel, and fully review how your product or service will look on that grade of paper. Once you decide on a paper grade, buy the amount of sheets you need to complete a catalog, and take it to the post office to get a price for bulk rate postage.

Be creative in your printing and paper purchasing

One catalog owner who mails out to members of a ham radio association receives a payment from the association when he prints his catalog, as long as he includes a letter from the association president, and the catalog looks to the members like another important benefit to them. Another catalog owner sells space advertisements from companies and organizations that sell related products and services, and these advertisements help pay for the thousands of catalogs he prints annually. Another catalog marketing owner in Massachusetts drop-ships his product to buyers from all over the country and sells his catalogs at a special price to his dealers. Figure 10-1 shows how the order card would be printed to give the dealer the image of being an important part of the business.

Notice how the "Mail to" section gives the dealer a special image, so the buyer can mail directly to the dealer and the dealer can have the product, in this case a book, shipped directly.

Another idea to get someone else to help you share the printing costs is to have the catalog owner bring in a partner and sell his or her products by the party plan. The partner splits the costs of the printing, so he or she is well supplied with current catalogs. Sometimes extra copies of your catalog can be used in

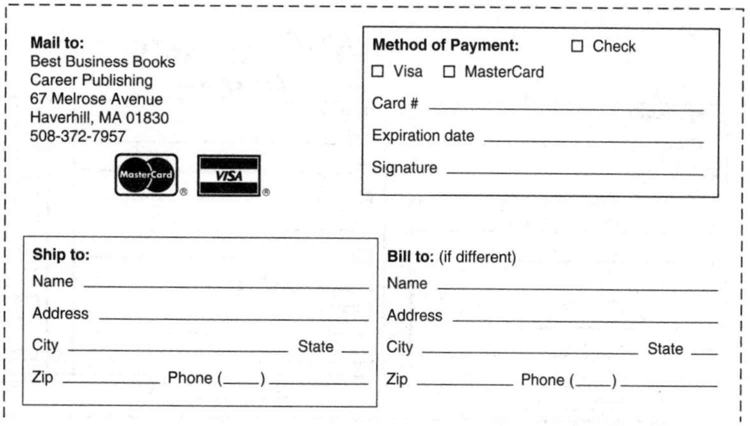
Mail to:
Best Business Books
Career Publishing
67 Melrose Avenue
Haverhill, MA 01830
508-372-7957

MasterCard® VISA®

Method of Payment: ☐ Check
☐ Visa ☐ MasterCard
Card # ______
Expiration date ______
Signature ______

Ship to:
Name ______
Address ______
City ______ State ___
Zip ______ Phone (___) ______

Bill to: (if different)
Name ______
Address ______
City ______ State ___
Zip ______ Phone (___) ______

Figure 10-1. Your order form should make it easy for your customer to complete it and send it back to you.

trade shows or to sell to retail stores. Two catalog owners located in the same location used the same grade of paper and purchased in large yearly lots at a large discount, and they even stored the paper at the same printer to save time and effort.

Consider your order form in your printing schedule

Sending out your catalogs without making it convenient for your prospects to order quickly and easily will result in few orders. Ask your printer whether she or he can print up envelope and order form inserts similar to the one in Fig. 10-2. Some companies specialize in printing only these envelope and order form inserts. One company in Massachusetts produced 1.6 billion catalog envelope and order form cards for mail order companies. Another way to get around purchasing these ordering inserts is to print the order form on the last page of your catalog and include a reply envelop within the catalog. In my first catalog I used the method of printing the order form on last page, directed my readers to use it, and included a separate envelope. Once your business grows you can think about purchasing the envelope and order form insert. Some catalog owners find that including additional order forms can increase orders. For example, if you mail catalogs to companies, and employees read the offers, enclosing extra copies of the order form will make it easier to order, and give you extra orders from the same catalog. One catalog owner

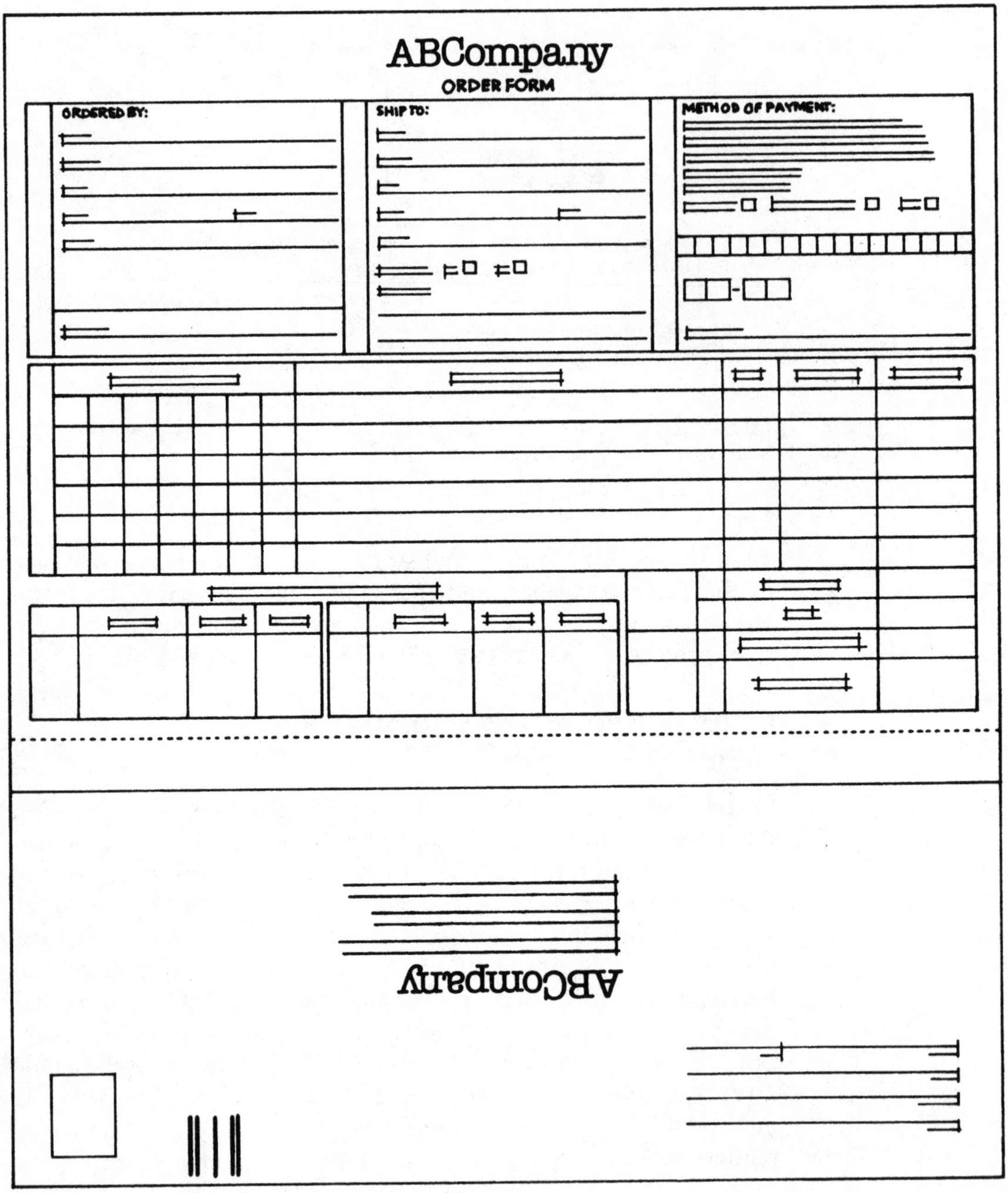

Figure 10-2. Order form. Your order form must be easy to ready and use, so your customers can order your products and services.

mails to prisoners in jail, and when extra order forms are enclosed, more sales are made, as the catalog is passed along to other prisoners.

Get a quote from your printer

One question which comes up regularly in my home-based catalog seminars is, Do you always hire the printer with the lowest quote? The answer is not always. You must evaluate the track record of the printer, the quality of his or her past work, the state-of-the-art equipment, proper facilities, the ability to complete the work on schedule, and the printer's experience in doing catalogs with your specifications. Avoid the problems which will result when you get only an oral quote for the printing job, and once it is completed, you get a bill for a much higher price.To avoid this problem a catalog gift and housewares owner focusing on European gifts uses a form shown in Fig. 10-3 which spells out all the costs involved in the finished catalog. Notice also, at the bottom of the quote, that you can have the printer include the full cost of the printing, and this should include any related sales tax or shipping costs so that there are no surprises when the job is completed. Make no corrections once your camera-ready artwork gets to the printer, because this will increase your costs substantially. For example, if you changed your mind on cover and switched it from a two-color to a four-color, expect to pay more than the original quote. Try to stay within your budget.

Examine your printing fully
before paying

Examine your printing fully before shipping it to your mailing house or to other dealers. There is no use paying for shipping and handling for printing when it does not meet your needs. Examine the printing fully, not just the top 25 to 50 catalogs on the top of the pile. Search down and do a sample check on each box of catalogs. The printer should have evaluated the work first, and the printer might not leave the faulty printed catalogs on top so you can review it. Take your time, and review each catalog fully. Make sure you have the correct quantity; let's say you printed 10,000 catalogs, and your printer put them into four boxes of 2500 each. Count one box and then check to see if the other three boxes are filled to the brim. Below you will find

QUOTATION FOR CATALOG PRINTING

Name _____ Date _____

Person to contact _____ Phone _____

Address _____

Job Name _____

Number of Pages _____ Same side _____ yes _____ no

Page size _____ Folded size _____ in. Quantity _____

Date camera-ready material to printer _____

Date needed _____

Paper weight _____ Color _____ Finish _____ Brand name _____

Miscellaneous instructions _____

_____

Ink colors _____ Front side _____ Other sides _____

Miscellaneous instructions _____

_____

Halftones _____ yes _____ no Diagram _____

Miscellaneous instructions _____

_____

Illustration _____ yes _____ no Drawing _____

** Quote for Printer
     My price for the above printing job, on date requested and the quantity stated, including folding, is $_____.

Signed _____

Date _____

Telephone _____

Figure 10-3. Quotation for catalog printing. Complete a quotation for each printing job. Ask the printer to sign it. Regularly compare the price to the quality. Watch your printing costs to increase your profits.

some things to consider before you accept the printing work for your catalog:

	Yes	No

- Do you have any smudges or double ink marks on certain words?
- Is the ink consistent all over the catalog?
- Did the printer include the artwork and photography for each page?
- Are the pages in the correct order?
- Are any letters broken or any words missing in the typography?
- Is this the paper you wanted to use?
- Is the final work something which meets your expectations?
- In your four-color work, does the color do your products justice?

Once you have filled out the evaluation above, use this when you go over the printing results with the printer. Use a business-like but firm manner. Never accept anything until the valuation is complete. If you take the printing home and discover a problem later, call the printer and take the job back to the printer as soon as possible. It will be very difficult to explain to the printer why you didn't mention the problem earlier. Never take out your checkbook and pay for some printing before you evaluate it on the points above. When you print up an economy catalog, with strictly black and white at a quick-print shop, be reasonable in what you expect for quality from the printer, for the economy price you will receive quick printing, which might not have the quality printing in more expensive color processing printing jobs.

Review the invoice fully, and check the invoice with the price on the quote you had signed by the printer. Read all figures, and make certain the quality and quantity are correct before you write your check.

How many copies of your catalog do you need?

Printing gets less expensive as you print additional copies. Your printer can give you a quote for 5000, 10,000, 15,000, 20,000 copies of your catalog. I recommend that in your first catalog printing you print 22,000 or 23,000 catalogs, so you can send

20,000 of them along to your preselected mailing lists and leave the remaining to be mailed to former customers, friends, business associates, classmates, association members, family members, or other business groups. You can save the extra catalogs for people who mail letters to you requesting a copy of your popular catalog. You might want to run a small advertisement urging people to buy or request your catalog; you need enough catalogs to keep mailing until you print another issue. The larger your catalog, the more expensive to go back to press. Don't print too many, but don't run short; this is the raw material of your business. You cannot sell from an empty wagon, and you cannot sell without catalogs.

Summary

Choose the type of printing job you need, whether it will be two-color, four-color, or black and white. Sometimes the four-color cover and black-and-white pages work for some catalog owners. Test various printing alternatives. Review your camera-ready artwork for organization and style. Choose the printer carefully; your printer becomes your important partner in this business. Give yourself enough time to print the job correctly, doing one printing job at a time. Give your printer the background of your business and your needs. Review the paper stock, buy it in quantity whenever possible. Use creative printing purchasing by selling catalogs to your dealer or mailing to association members. Use the drop-shipping method with dealers. Remember to print your order form and envelope. Get a quote and ask your printer to sign it. Examine your printing job before paying for it. Print more copies than you expect to use, especially on your first catalog; you will find many ways to use them. Avoid running short; your business is catalogs, so you need to have enough on hand.

11

Mailing lists

Your own mailing list, which contains the correct name and address of customers or potential customers, will become the most valuable asset in your business. Your own mailing list is called a "house list," which means these are your customers who have purchased products and services from you in the past. The people on your house list are like family because they trusted you and your company by taking out their checkbooks and sending you an order. You must develop strategies and an attractive catalog with quality products and services to keep your customers buying, not just for 6 months or a few years, but for life.

You can rent names from ABC Company to mail out your catalogs, and even though the ABC Company list has an excellent reputation, nothing will out-pull your own house mailing list. Review below a test of three mailing lists, mailing one using your house list and two using rented lists.

Test of Mailing Lists

Date mailed	No. mailed	List type	No. of sales	Percent of mailing	Total sales
1/2/99	2000	House	200	10	$8000
1/2/99	2000	Rental	40	2	1600
1/3/99	2000	Rental	60	3	2400

A rented list, rented for one use only, usually has 2000 to 5000 names, and no copies can be made of that list to be used later.

One of my popular questions in the catalog seminar is, How can the list owner check to see if the renter of the list is making copies of the names on the list to be used later? List owners "salt" the lists, which means they put in names of people who will keep a list of mailings to them, and then they check the companies which in fact, rented the list. They know who is using the list without paying rental costs. I don't recommend making copies of rented mailing lists—many catalog owners earn a portion of their income from this operation, and you might decide to rent your own mailing list in the future. Don't rent out a mailing list until you have been in the business for a few years. Your goal in the beginning is to build up your house list.

How do you build your own list?

One of the best ways to start your house list is to include all your current customers in your present business. People who have purchased from you in the past you can get from your own sales records. You can also get names from small-space advertising in magazines of interest to your market. For example, let's say you are selling bridal products; you would want to advertise in a magazine read by future brides and offer your catalog free if requested by a specific time. You might want to offer a free sample if your prospect requests a catalog. Remember, you want to get people interested in your products or services, not just someone who enjoys reading catalogs. Below you will find some sources to increase your house list.

Sources to Build Your House Mailing List
1. Your present customers
2. Inquiries from small-space advertising
3. Dealer lists
4. Telephone inquiries
5. Customer recommendations
6. Chamber of commerce directories
7. Trade show attendees
8. Friends, classmates, relatives

Your goal will be to take a name and convert it from just a name into a buyer. I recommend that you separate the buyer from the inquiree who simply asks for a catalog but does not buy. Below you will notice how I keyed the address so I will know the difference between the inquiree (*I*), and the buyer (*B*): next to the letter *I* is included the date 1/99, January 1999, and the letters *PM* for *Popular Mechanics*, the source of the inquiry.

Address label	(*I*) 1/99 *PM*	(*B*) 2/99 *CM-SI*
	William F. Kreeper	Corienne A. Mack
	10 Fowler St.	25 Apple Rd.
	Boston, MA 00001	Las Vegas, NV 10000

CM-SI stands for a catalog mailing using the *Sports Illustrated* rental list. You build up your house list by two basic methods: mailing out catalogs to people who ask for a catalog once they read your space advertisement in, say, *Changing Times* magazine, or mailing out catalogs to a preselected rented mailing list. Review your sales on a regular basis to determine whether you are getting your orders from those small-space advertisements or in your mailings. How do you do it? Good question. Testing on a regular basis is how you determine where your orders come from, and your main tool to discover where the sale originated is to key the order form. Some catalog owners key by putting in letters, say, *CT,* for *Changing Times* space advertisement, and *CFO* for catalog mailing using the *Chief Financial Officer* mailing list. Below you will see an example of both keys in your address next to suite, to determine the sales origination of your orders. Other catalog owners do all their keying on the address label on the catalog itself and request the buyer to use the address label when ordering.

MAIL TO:	**MAIL TO:**
Executive Catalog Co.	Executive Catalog Co.
10 Melrose Ave., Suite *CT*	10 Melrose Ave., Suite *CFO*
New York, NY 10000	New York, NY 10000

Run a test to determine just where your sales are originating, and then continue to advertise in that magazine or that mailing list. Below you will find a test to determine which is the best advertising method for you.

Date	Magazine	Mailing list	No. of sales	Sale per order	Total sales
Jan. 1999	*Changing Times*		100	$34	$3400
Jan. 1999		Doctors list	73	30	2190
Difference			27		$1210

The *Changing Times* space advertising program in January gave you 100 new buyers to add to your house list, and the mailing to the rented doctors list only gave you 73 additional buyers to add to the most important list, your own house list. The *Changing Times* space advertisement gave you more sales dollars versus the mailing list advertising, but when you concentrate on building your house list, the buyers are the most important element to you. You will make your money not on your first order to the new buyer, but month after month, year after year, when you reach that objective to keep your buyers for life.

How do you choose a mailing list?

You choose a mailing list by selecting people who have the interest, desire, and purchasing power, the money to buy products and services from your catalog. Your mailing list can be your target market. You want people who buy by mail, people who enjoy shopping by catalog and are willing to continue buying from other catalogs you send. There are two different types of mailing lists, the mail response mailing list and the compiled mailing list. The mail response list offers names and addresses of people who purchased products and services by mail within the last 6 months or one year. Naturally you want to select people who just purchased a VCR 30 to 60 days ago, so you can sell them supplies for the VCR, and you want to market those individuals when they are in the mood to buy. Don't let buyers wait; they might cool down and stop buying. Give the buyer reasons to continue purchasing, and from your catalog. Below you will find just a sample of mail response mailing lists available to rent within a few weeks, or you can schedule the rental the day your catalog is printed.

Mail Response Mailing Lists

Buyers of personal computers

Woman's clothing mail order buyers

Subscribers to teen magazines

Book buyers of home improvement material

Business supplies buyers

Computer machine subscribers

Coin mail order buyers

Gift buyers by mail order

Gourmet Magazine subscribers

Farm Magazine subscribers

Photography equipment buyers

Romance book buyers

Beauty and diet buyers

Hobby and craft mail order buyers

Compiled Mailing Lists

Catalog mail order houses	Computer stores
Sports medicine clinics	Plumbing contractors
Taxation attorneys	Craft enthusiasts
Hand surgeons	Fish tackle dealers
Vascular surgeons	Food brokers
Heads of household by income	Female professionals
Art museums	Fax machine owners
Children by age	Golf and country clubs
Elks Club members	Stock market investors
Women's clothing	Purchasing agents
Mail order firms	Pension fund attorneys
Ham radio clubs	Dermatologists
America's most wealthy people	Adding machine dealers
Antique dealers	

The compiled list is not as strong as the mail response list because some of these people have not purchased by mail recently. The compiled list offers names of individuals with something in common, such as the same occupation or in a related business such as computers, or belonging to the same organization such as the Kiwanis Club. The compiled list can work when you send a unique catalog which offers products and services different from competing catalogs.

Choose a mailing list which reaches your target market

Earlier in the book we discussed selecting your market; now go back to Chapter 5 and review your notes for the most desirable target market for your catalog offerings. Avoid falling into the trap of selecting a mailing list because you like the title of it, or think it just might work; rather, focus on your target market. Look up mailing lists companies in the city telephone directory and ask for a copy of their latest mailing lists catalog. Review it completely; the mail-directed lists as well as the compiled lists will give you many ideas. Call the Best Mailing List Company at 800-692-2378 and ask them to send you their latest catalog. They will be happy to mail one out to you.

Be creative in your list selection

Just because you decided on renting a list of mail order gift buyers does not mean you will just take a list of 5000 buyers from all over the country. With the advent of computer technology you can sort that 5000 names by the following:

Possible Selects for Mailing Lists

- Gender
- Occupation
- Income
- Zip code
- Time since last purchase—30, 90, 180 days
- Amount of purchase
- 5-mile radius of zip code
- Purchases by credit cards
- Purchases by cash

Once you get the basic list idea, call the mailing list company. Most will give you free consultation, so ask how they can select the best possible list for you. The basic list is similar to a chocolate cake mix, and the special selections, such as by income or by time of last purchase, become the frosting on the cake. Once you find a list which works for you, go back to it over and over and roll it out to the end. For example, you find a gift buyer list which works for the first 10,000 names—the total list is 200,000 names; you can keep mailing your catalog to get the maximum sales. Below is an example of a mailing list test and then a projection of what you could possibly earn by rolling it out to the end of the list. As you roll it out you also increase your house list, which is very important to your success.

Date	Gift buyers list	Cost per 1000	Cost of list rental	Responses	No. of orders	Average amt. per order	Total sales
Mar. 1999	10,000	$70.00	$ 700	2%	200	$37	$7,400
1999	190,000	70.00	13,300	2	3,800	37	110,600
Total	200,000		$20,300		5,800		$118,000

Your list rental will be $20,300 to send your catalog to the full 200,000 names, but you will gain sales of $118,000 and can now add 5800 names to your house list. You can now mail to them free of all list rental costs; they are now your property, and you can rent them out to others in the future. A good response rate is anything above 1.5 percent, or 0.015 of your total mailing. Don't forget the other costs which relate to the direct mailing of your catalog: your printing costs of your catalog, outside envelope, postage, the list rental cost, the mailing cost of assembling catalog for mailing, and the cost of the products and services sold. You will get some returns, people who are not happy with the product, as all catalog owners have experienced; you can get up to 5 percent returns, especially when you mail or sell to a new list.

Use a list broker

Many catalog and mail order owners turn the list selection process over to a specialist called the "list broker." This specialist has knowledge of the field, and once you give him or her a copy of your catalog and offer details on your target market, you can review a number of possibilities. Remember, you make the final decision. Avoid spending too much of your list broker's time; get the information and then decide. Always do a test of a large list before ordering 20,000 to 50,000 names. Below you will find a sample letter you can send to your broker or mailing list company to get some ideas from them.

Letter to Mailing List Broker

March 5, 1999

Ms. Jennifer Beals
Oxford Mailing List Brokers
10 Main
Salem, Oregon 10001

Dear Ms. Beals:

I just completed my plans to print and mail my 22-page catalog to mail order gift buyers. I would like a test selection of 5000 gift mail order names, selected with last purchased date within 90 days, with $40,000 yearly income, and who purchased gifts by credit card. Total list should be at least 100,000 names.

Please send me any information available on the above-named list and selects. I can be reached at 508-999-4440 from 8 a.m. to 7 p.m. daily.
Thank you.

MARY HOWLAND
PRESIDENT

P.S. My printed catalog will be sent to you.

Make your mailing list broker your business partner by giving him or her all the information about products, offers, success with other magazines, lists, or other marketing methods.

Choose a format

Once you select a list and determine what format you need, you can get the list sent to you with the names printed on pressure-sensitive labels, whereby you can simply remove and place them on your catalogs for mailing. Catalog marketing owners who decide to have their catalogs sent by a mailing service can have their list printed on 4-across Cheshire or continuous computer paper. The labels are affixed to your catalog or envelope by a Cheshire machine, which cuts the page into label segments and applies glue, and the catalog is now ready for mailing.

Why does the mailing list owner or list broker want to see your catalog or mailing piece? The list owner or broker wants to avoid renting to the same mailers; they strive to give the people on the list a variety of owners. Some list owners want to avoid renting their list to a direct competitor. By reviewing the catalog, they can determine the quality of your products and services. Looking at your catalog fully prevents rentals to illegal mail order operators and avoids involvement with illegal products and services.

Strive for security of your house list

Since your list is the most important asset in your business, do not leave it unattended in a meeting, at the printer's, mailer's, or other public place. Keep it in a locked drawer or safe. Never just loan your mailing list cards, disks, or tapes overnight. Your whole business is in your house list. Practice a sense of security consciousness at home and away from home. If you choose to rent out your list, get paid for it; avoid giving your assets away.

Mailing lists age quickly

Businesses change, industries change, consumers' tastes change, and so do mailing lists. People move, die, get transferred out of state, or for one reason or another change their place of residence. Statistics on mailing lists show that a mailing list at least one year old is only 25 to 30 percent accurate. In other words, with a mailing list of 10,000 names, 2500 would have moved away, and your catalogs might not reach those individuals. You must take action to keep your list up to date.

Ask your customers to please read the label on the catalog to verify the name, address, and zip code. Ask them to make any changes and send the label back to you. Make the changes immediately. Another method is to ask the postal service to help you by stating "Address Correction Requested" on the upper left corner of your envelope, under your name and address; the postal service will for a fee give you the new address.

Duplication of names is another important consideration for you. Some mailers use the "merge-and-purge" system where the magnetic tapes compare the names on your list with the names on a rented list and with all the other lists within the mailing list service organization. The goal will be to give you one list, without duplications. This system will help you save many thousands of dollars when you do mailings on a regular basis. Some catalog owners like duplication of names for heavy users—to keep offering them their catalog offerings.

When do you take a name from your house list?

You take people off your list when they move away and you cannot get their new addresses and when people no longer buy your product or service. You play the role of a salesperson, you keep presenting your product, and when you continue to get turned down catalog after catalog, you cut your losses and drop the former customer. One catalog owner from Missouri uses a point basis for each customer. Five points are given if a customer purchased during the last six months, 2 points for six months to one year; 1 point is given for each hundred dollars of sales; if a name does not reach 7 points, the name is dropped from the list. Catalog marketers cannot assume mailing, list rental, and printing costs with no orders from your house list.

Each mailing list has a profile

The best mailing list should be a mirror of your target market. Remember how you visualized the best possible prospect for your product? You designed a profile which carefully fitted together demographics and psychographics to round it out. In my own catalog marketing business, I have a house list which has a profile of my customers which includes the following:

> Education: high school 40 percent, 55 percent with at least some college or a degree

Income: household income: $65,000 to $80,000 yearly

Occupation: White-collar professionals, supervisors, managers, salespeople, business owners, home-based business owners

Product or service: Business books, home-based books, how-to manuals, seminars, courses, reports, and newsletters

Age: 25 to 55 years old

Geographic location: Worldwide, 95 percent in the United States

You get this information by sticking close to your customers, sending them questionnaires, checking the source of your sales. Did you get that response from *Stereo Magazine, U.S. News and World Report, Sports Illustrated?* Each one offers you information on the demographics of their publication. Check each mailing list completely to see if it has the profile of prospects which you feel will buy your product.

Summary

Mailing lists help you to reach your target market. Lists are rented for one time only, and your house list is important to build for your success. Each order and inquiry can add to your house list. Test lists and determine where you obtained each order. You can choose from a mail response or compiled list. Remember that lists age quickly, so get rid of names of customers who move or refuse to order for a long time. Some catalog owners merge and purge their lists to avoid excessive duplication. Keep your list secure by keeping it locked up, and don't loan it out. Know the profile of your customers.

12

Mailing out your catalog

When you walked into your home office, you nearly tripped over the boxes of 10,000 catalogs, recently printed. Your desk is covered with your recently rented mailing list of 10,000 names. I recommend to my students and catalog marketing owners in the beginning to mail their own catalogs themselves. I recommend this to give you the experience of doing the mailing, so you can understand the process fully. If you decide to hire a mailing firm for your business in the future, you will know how to evaluate this service.

Your post office is your business partner

Although there are many stories about the competence and motivation of the postal service, on the whole the price of a stamp is small compared to the overall service delivered. Stop at your local or regional post office and introduce yourself to the supervisor or postmaster. Tell her or him your plans to use the postal service for your multiple mailings in your business.

The regional post office in your area gives periodic seminars to business mailers like yourself, and information is shared on rates and mailing forms; supplies are given such as boxes for bulk mailings, rubber bands, and stickers. The post office knows that catalog and mail order owners are heavy users of their services and that helping them helps the postal service earn more money. The postal service also issues a free catalog for mailers to keep up with the latest changes in mailings; it is called "Memo to Mailers," and your first issue can be obtained by writing directly to: Memo for Mailer, P.O. Box 1, Linwood, New Jersey, 07221.

Review other delivery options

There are other small-package delivery services, and some of their services and prices are competitive to the postal service. Review these services and give them full consideration. Many delivery services cannot deliver to the post office boxes, because these boxes are operated by the U.S. Postal Service. Extra services such as a pickup at your home are offered by some delivery companies, and some delivery services even will prepare the envelopes or boxes for your catalog or products.

Do you need extra supplies or a post office box?

Very few supplies are needed to do your own mailing. Invest in a small postal scale. You will need a box to put the catalogs away once you separate them, but for the complete mailing everything you will need will be given to you by the post office, such as rubber bands and stickers for bulk mailings.

In the beginning of your business I recommend that you rent a small box for the first six months. You can check your mail daily; stop in any time of day from 7 a.m. to 6 p.m. You will avoid getting your personal mail at home mixed in with your catalog business mail. As your business grows you can ask for a larger mailbox to handle additional mail, and you will get some returns as well; the post office will hold them for you and leave a note in your mailbox that a large box is waiting for you. By your having a post office box, the returns are kept at the post office rather than at your mailbox or door step at home.

Learn about the various postal rates

First class is used only when you need quick delivery of your catalog or delivery within two or three days. Many catalog owners use this for payment of invoices and urgent requests for a catalog, with high expectation of an order. First class is faster and has fewer restrictions and will be returned to you when it is undelivered. Many catalog owners use the first class when they are sending out a few catalogs at a time and when time is a high priority. For the larger mailings, the bulk rate class is used, saving a substantial amount of money.

A bulk rate permit is given to you when you file Form 3601 and pay a one-time fee, as long as you use the bulk rate service within 12 months. If the post office finds you are not using the bulk rate offer, they can cancel it on you. The additional fee is the annual fee for the special bulk rate. Remember, all pieces must be of identical size and weight, and 200 pieces must be mailed at once, sorted correctly. You save money by doing the sorting, and this savings could be thousands of dollars each year. Using the bulk rate, your catalogs or mail will not get to the prospects as fast as first class, but catalogs can be mailed across the country in a week or 10 days.

In order to sort correctly, you want to make four packages: one for all catalogs addressed to the same zip code, a second package of catalogs with the same 3 digits in the zip code, such as 019, a third package includes remaining catalogs addressed to the same state, and the fourth package will include all remaining pieces and will be called the "mixed states packages." (See Fig. 12-1.) The top catalog will have a pressure-sensitive sticker to help the postal service people process the catalogs faster. (See Fig. 12-2.) This may seem like a great deal of work right now, but you will find it easy and worth the savings. Remember, sort by 10 or more pieces, put an elastic band on them, and place them into the boxes supplied from the post office to bring them down to the post office for mailing. Make sure the sorting is done correctly, or the post office will not ship your catalogs at the special rate.

How do you pay for the bulk mailing? Your post office will accept a check for the cost of your bulk mailing once you fill out the necessary paperwork for your mailing. File PS Form 3602 when you have your permit number on your mailing pieces and PS Form 3602PC when you use meter stamp mailings. Make sure you have the permit number printed on your mailing piece or catalog at the printer. Your permit number will be printed on your catalog just like Fig. 12-2.

Use your bulk mailing permit regularly. Not only will you save a great deal of money but you will sell regularly as well, as your customers will enjoy hearing from you and seeing your new offers. When you mail your bulk mailing, include yourself in the mailing, so you can read the catalog and react to the presentation just like another customer.

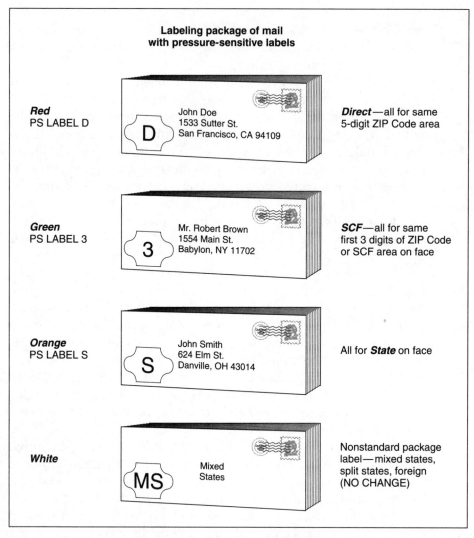

**Labeling package of mail
with pressure-sensitive labels**

Red
PS LABEL D

D

John Doe
1533 Sutter St.
San Francisco, CA 94109

Direct—all for same
5-digit ZIP Code area

Green
PS LABEL 3

3

Mr. Robert Brown
1554 Main St.
Babylon, NY 11702

SCF—all for same
first 3 digits of ZIP Code
or SCF area on face

Orange
PS LABEL S

S

John Smith
624 Elm St.
Danville, OH 43014

All for **State** on face

White

MS

Mixed
States

Nonstandard package
label—mixed states,
split states, foreign
(NO CHANGE)

Figure 12-1. Put labels on mail for special bulk rates. The four different labels can be attached to the top mailing piece of each mailing package. These labels are available free from your local post office.

Check your costs before printing. To save yourself the extra costs, prepare a dummy of your complete catalog, using the paper you intend to use in your finished catalog and take it to the post office. Include all dummy memos, letters, and order forms and the outside envelope; ask the post office for their approval and the price for each catalog mailed, both for first-class mail and for bulk rate. Sometimes an extra page or two can

```
┌─────────────────────────┐
│                         │
│      BULK RATE          │
│    U.S. POSTAGE         │
│       PAID              │
│    BOSTON, MA.          │
│    PERMIT No. 1         │
│                         │
└─────────────────────────┘
```

Figure 12-2. Make certain your bulk rate permit is included on your catalog before printing it to save time and effort.

move the catalog into another higher rate class. The postal regulations and authorities can change, so checking out costs will help to establish your postage budget.

How would you handle inquiries for your catalog?

Some catalog marketers will send out single copies of their catalogs to people who write and call requesting a copy of their catalog. When you wait too long before sending the catalog, the potential customer gets impatient and buys from another competitor. When the catalog is sent by first-class postage, the cost of postage will increase, but you cannot get the sale unless the catalog is sent out quickly.

Do you charge for the catalog?

When we discuss the cost of preparation of putting together the catalog and of the related postage, a common reaction is whether to charge for the catalog. The answer is not in the beginning of your business—you want to try to get your catalog in as many hands as possible to maximize your sales. A well-known magazine, *Catalog of Catalogs,* offers catalog marketing owners a free listing of their catalog, and once you get listed in this publication, many requests will be mailed to you asking for copies of your catalogs. Test the sales attained for mailing out to the people who read this catalog of publications. Remember, some of these people may just want to collect these catalogs and not buy from you. When you do your test and you determine that very few catalogs are sold to this group, you might consider charging this group, $1, $2, or $3 for your catalog to help defray your costs. Some catalog owners charge for their catalog but offer the cost of the catalog, let's say $2, as a refundable when people purchase something from the catalog.

Mail early in the day

Whether you are doing a bulk mailing or sending out catalogs for people who inquired about a copy of your catalog, mail early in the day. The bulk mailing which arrives just before the post office closes at 5 p.m. will not be processed until the next day and may not move out of your post office for another full day. Give the postal employees a chance to get started immediately on your mailing by mailing early.

Mail out your catalog when you ship a product

Fred Smith purchased a gift item from your small-space advertisement in *Yankee Magazine,* and when you mailed it to him, you also included a copy of your latest gift catalog. This process is called "bounce-back selling," because you are trying to sell current customers, the easiest people to sell, by giving them a wider assortment of products. Never hide the fact you have your own catalog; keep copies in your car—when someone asks about your catalog, tell them you would be happy to give them a complimentary catalog and that you would handle their order personally. One catalog owner from Massachusetts was recently on a radio show and was discussing his catalog business; at the end of the show, with the approval of the host of the show he said, "I will be happy to send a copy of the Best Gift Catalog if your listeners will send me a large envelope and two first class stamps. I look forward to hearing from them." Notice how the catalog owner made the free catalog offer at the end of the show, when the listeners wanted more information. The catalog owner asked for an envelope with postage on it, and saved both the postage, envelope, and addressing costs, which are paid by the prospect. The only costs for the catalog marketer would be the cost of the catalog.

Test your mailing results regularly

In order to determine what offers are working, you must test and evaluate the mailings which bring in the orders. Did you get the sale from a rental list? A small-space advertisement? A special public relations program on a local radio show? A house list? By testing you will be able to continue using the very best list possible. The following shows how to keep track of mailings:

Date	Mailing list used	Amt. mailed	Amt. of orders	Total sales
Feb. 15	ABC Co.	10,000	200	$8000
Feb. 28	Newsletter list	10,000	210	8050
March 1	Mail order buyers	10,000	220	8800
March 15	House list	10,000	250	9500

Lists change over time, people change, products run their cycle, services also are viewed differently over a long period of time, so remember to review your mailing list selection.

What is a first-class permit?

This is a special service provided by the postal service through which you can offer your prospects free postage when they send you the order. A copy of a first-class permit is shown in Fig. 12-3. This first-class print must be printed on your envelopes; to take advantage of it, the service must be communicated to your customers in the catalog.

The advantage of this permit is that the customer can send you an order right away without waiting to obtain the necessary postage stamps. The disadvantage is the cost, since you must purchase the first-class permit from the post office and pay for each envelope sent to you at the post office. Unfortunately some

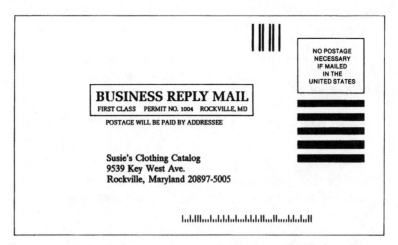

Figure 12-3. First-class permit. A first-class permit gives your customers the convenience of sending you an order without paying the postage.

people send their envelopes back empty or with a message which make no sense, and you are obligated to pay for them, just like the envelope with the check in there. Many catalog owners are using regular reply envelopes, which requires the customers to pay for their own postage.

Mail your catalogs with the personal approach

When you mail your catalog, include a small note or letter to your prospects that you enjoy their interest in your product or service and that you really care about serving them. It can be a small note, like the one below, but it serves as an important method to start the customer service process. People like to feel that their business and interest in you and your product count to you. It is similar to sitting at a local restaurant, while waiting for your food, and the owner of the restaurant stops by to say "Hi, how are you today, Mary?" I'm happy you stopped in today. Have a nice day." What a great feeling you get, when you're treated this way. It doesn't matter if you're alone or with an important guest, the feeling is just very nice. Treat your customer as a very important person.

From the Desk of Sylvia Burbank

Dear Customer:

Thank you for your recent order. I have enclosed our recent catalog, and I am delighted to feature our latest gourmet foods from Portland, Maine.

A few years ago, when my friend Susan and I started this business, we committed ourselves to the highest customer service in the business.

We'd like to serve you, so if you have any questions, comments, or ideas, please drop us a line. Enjoy your catalog.

SYLVIA BURBANK

Some catalog professionals contend that a personal letter can increase your response rate to over 20 percent, especially to a new prospect. Strive to make your letter as personal as possible.

Give your mailing sufficient time to work

Once you get your catalogs into the mail, give the process enough time to work fully. When you do a bulk mailing some of those catalogs will be moving to other parts of the country, perhaps Maine or California, and it takes time. You will usually get your first order in a week or 10 days after mailing, and for the next few weeks the orders will be stronger, until the flow gradually slows up. The response to your mailing is similar to a teacher giving you a grade for a course in school—your grade is basically the result of how hard you worked during the class term. In the catalog marketing business, the success of your mailing is the result of how you selected your products or services, how you segmented your market, and how you tailored an offer with the best price, terms, and personal approach possible. When you find that your mailing is profitable, don't change anything and continue with that set of strategies until it stops working, then make the necessary changes to get back into the profitable column again.

Do you mail to foreign countries?

Many catalog marketers hesitate to mail to foreign countries because of the extra cost for postage. We live in a global economy. Other catalog owners charge foreign prospects for their catalogs to offset some cost of printing and mailing out. You might want to do a test to see whether foreign prospects want to buy from your catalog. Many foreigners enjoy catalogs and direct mail. One catalog owner from Texas started selling a few of her catalog products by magazine, and, since the magazine was sold internationally, many customers from France, Hong Kong, and Sweden responded. These inquiries turned into customers and were added to the house list. Now once yearly a catalog is sent to these customers all over the world. Watch out for excessive shipping costs. Ask your foreign customers to pay you with money orders, payable in U.S. funds.

Mail to your house list often

Good catalog marketers make it a point to mail at least six times a year to their house list. The catalog marketers with the most success send out smaller versions of their catalog, focusing on seasonal products or services for the customers. Other catalog owners send out one catalog each year with the theme "Cleaning Out Overstock," and this catalog gives special prices to move products.

Since your catalog is really a salesperson for you in the prospect's home or business, the more calls or mailings you make, the better your chances to make the sale. Your customers enjoy your presentations, and even if you fail to get an order, your catalog has been read and evaluated; perhaps an order will be sent to you at a later date. Keep sending your catalogs to your house list to keep prospects' interest.

Summary

Mailing your catalog is one of the most enjoyable aspects of the catalog marketing business. Doing the mailing yourself in the beginning of your business will give you valuable experience in the mailing. Let your post office become your business partner. Use the knowledge, experience, free supplies, and free newsletter offered by the postal service. There are other delivery services available to you, including getting your own post office box. Learn the postal class rates: The bulk rate saves you a great deal of money and still delivers your catalogs at reasonable time limits. You can get your bulk rate permit at the post office. Check your weight costs before you print and mail. Handle your inquiries accurately and promptly to increase your orders. You make the decision to charge or offer your catalog free—test your results of charging versus offering your catalog free. Mail your catalogs early in the day. Mail out your new catalog when you ship a product to a customer. Keep the customer buying. Test your mailing results regularly. Consider using first-class permits to increase orders. Attempt to make the personal approach with each mailing, because customers want to feel you care about customers, not names on a computerized list. Keep mailing to your house list. Give your mailing time to work.

13

Handling inquiries and orders professionally

You will get telephone calls, postcards, formal letters, fax messages, and handwritten letters requesting information or some assistance. Sometimes the request will be as simple as a request for your latest catalog. Other requests will ask about a particular product or service or raise some question about your catalog field. For example, one catalog marketing owner gets many letters requesting information on how to purchase difficult-to-find tools, and each letter gives the owner important information on future products and what the customers are looking for today. Treat each inquiry as an essential part of your business—this inquiry is the beginning of the buying process. Give prospects all the information they need to solve their problems and make it easy for them to buy from you.

Test other catalog companies for their inquiry-handling techniques before you print up your first catalog. Call some catalog companies using their 800 numbers and ask them to send you their latest catalogs. Make notes of how they handle your call. Did they ask you any questions? Did they ask you if you wanted to be included on their mailing list? Did they ask you how you learned of them? Did they give you a feeling they really wanted your business? Did they mail out your catalog immediately? Did they do as they promised? Do you feel they laid the foundation for a strong future relationship? Did they work hard enough to earn your business? Mail some postcards to catalog owners requesting a copy of their catalog as well. For a listing of catalogs mail to: *The Catalog Handbook,* 1020 N. Broadway, Suite 111, Milwaukee, WI 53202. Keep a note pad of how much time it takes to receive catalogs. Did the catalog companies send you any additional information or catalogs after the initial inquiry? You will learn a great deal from doing your own inquiry testing. Incorporate any special techniques you liked into your own inquiry methods.

The best catalog owners give the very best customer service

How you handle the inquiry is a sign of how you will handle your customer service program in your business. Good customer service means you care about the customers and prospects in your business, and your goal is to work continually toward converting the prospects into satisfied customers. The top catalog owners know the value of treating customers professionally and giving individual attention to each one.

Set up your own inquiry response system. One catalog owner developed a section of his office at home for the proper handling of inquiries by mail. He calls the system the 4 *W*s system, and following it correctly means knowing the 4 *W*s: *Who, What, Why,* and *When. Who* is inquiring? Get the full name and address. *What* information does the individual need? Make certain you send it. *Why* did the customers respond to you? Did they read about your catalog in a magazine? Did they hear about it from a friend? Did they buy a product from you in the past? When did they learn about your catalog? The answers to the above questions give you valuable information to add to your inquiry record, as shown in Fig. 13-1. Review these inquiry records regularly to get a feel for the type of individual who is interested in reviewing your catalog and considering your products or services for possible purchase. Keep a record of all inquiries, and not just some of them; this information is essential to selling and growing in this business.

| Name ———————————————————————————— |
| Address ———————————————————————————— |
| City ——————— State——————— Zip ——————— |

Date rec'd	Advertisement	Magazine	Catalog/ material shipped	Date follow-up catalog/ material
————	—————	————	————	————

Date order received	No.	Value
———————	————	$————
———————	————	$————
———————	————	$————

Products of interest ——————————————————————

Date entered on mailing list ————————————————

Comments ——————————————————————————

————————————————————————————————

Second follow-up date ————————————————————

————————————————————————————————

Figure 13-1. Catalog inquiry record. Keeping a record of your catalog inquiries gives you important information about which rental list, magazine, or special offer is working to give you the necessary sales to succeed.

Mail the information or catalog immediately

Nothing helps your sales and profits more than prompt attention to the mailing of the catalog to the person requesting it. Beat the competition by getting your catalog to the mailbox of your potential customer. Strike when the iron is hot. Once the prospect responds, your chances increase by acting immediately; when you wait, the prospect might change his or her mind and buy from your competitor. Send out the catalog by first-class mail.

Go the extra mile for your prospect

Scott Smith of Vermont writes to you and requests information on the new pottery supplies line of your new catalog. He has never seen your catalog. Rather than just sending out the catalog and letting him find the products in this large catalog, you send a personal note, directing him to the section and page of the catalog to help increase the sale. Your note could be as simple as:

> Thank you for your recent letter on pottery supplies. You will find a full assortment on pages 18–22. Please call me at 999-888-7719 if you have any questions, comments, or ideas. Thanks for your interest.
>   Regards,
>
>   BETTY CLARK

Too often catalog owners know their catalogs so well that they assume the prospects will be able to use the catalog without any extra help. Never assume anything; make every effort to assist your prospects to buy from you.

Design a system for others to follow

You know how to fulfill the needs of your inquiries, but you must also set up a system so that others in your company or family can do it. In the days of empowered employees, a system for inquiry handling is essential. For example, Lynn Gordon of Pennsylvania, a lamp catalog owner, is away from her office because she participates in a number of shows all over the country. Lynn set up an inquiry handling procedure which is placed above the inquiry desk. It includes the following:

1. List name of catalog requested.
2. Indicate what advertisement or lead generated the inquiry.
3. Put prospect's name on mailing list, make out inquiry records.
4. Mail catalog or other information by first-class mail immediately.

Lynn found that prior to developing a system which any of her family members or prospects could understand, many catalogs or requested information were sent but not on a timely basis. Using this system Lynn has built her home mailing list to over 10,000 names.

The following is a *fast method to respond to inquiries:* You received 20 letters requesting catalogs, and you want to respond quickly; one way to do this is to cut out the name and address right from the envelope, then glue or put tape on your catalog or catalog envelope, and mail it out. Make certain you keep a copy of the letter with the full name and address on it to record on your inquiry record and put on your mailing list.

You can get other inquiries by attending trade shows, speaking at group service or club meetings in your area, or getting on your local radio or cable television shows. Let people know you are in the business, so they can read and order from your catalog. These methods will be discussed in the next chapter.

It is very expensive to continually respond to your inquiries and receive a poor sales response. Many people with inquiries just want to turn the pages of your catalog and dream but not respond to your offer. Many people like to collect catalogs rather than buy from them. Test your inquiries by determining what prospects are buying from you. Review the test below:

Date	No. of inquiries	No. converted	Percentage	Source
February	300	30	10	10 *Popular Mechanics* ad 15 *Yankee* ad 5 guest on radio show

Ask yourself why you received the latest sale. What turned the process into a sale? Keep working hard to convert those prospects into lifelong buyers.

Handle orders successfully

Many of the same principles of inquiry handling apply to sending out orders to your customers. Nothing is more beneficial than shipping promptly, and nothing is more detrimental than delaying shipment to your new customer. Treat new customers as very important people. Customers expect prompt, professional service, and when this is missing they feel rejected.

When you cannot ship an order in a timely manner, write back to the customer quickly and give the reason for the delay. Your message could be as simple as the following:

Dear Ms. Jones:

Thanks for your order of our latest book, *Career Skills,* last week.

We are out of stock and expect a reprinting in 2 weeks. Would you like to substitute another book, receive a refund check, or are you willing to wait the 2 weeks? Please let me know as soon as possible by calling me at 212-999-0001.

Thank you,

FRED ALLENHURST
PRESIDENT

The Federal Trade Commission requires you to notify your customers within 30 days after the order is placed when you cannot fulfill their order. The customer will get nervous when you fail to respond and might cancel the order or, worse, avoid buying from you in the future. The Federal Trade Commission will fine catalog and mail order companies that fail to comply with this important rule.

Summary

Inquiries come to you in all forms—postcards, letters, telephone calls, faxes, and formally typed letters. Respond correctly to all of them. Investigate how other catalog owners handle inquiries—top catalog companies take good care of their inquiries. Set up your own system to mail out inquiries and orders immediately. Do the extra for your prospects. Design a system for others to follow. Review methods to get inquiries. Review the percentage of people with inquiries who become buyers. When you cannot ship promptly, call or write to your buyer—this is the federal law.

14

Profitable public relations for your business

When you read your local newspaper, scan a magazine, or watch your favorite radio or television show, the people and the subjects of those shows, the articles and features are the result of public relations. Someone convinced the local newspaper editor to run the favorable article. What is public relations? It is a set of activities by a business or agent working with the media, including the newspapers, newsletters, radio, and television stations, to obtain a favorable review of their products or services to educate the public about your business or organization.

The exciting element about public relations is that you will get valuable exposure about your catalog business, or your mail order business, and about yourself for free. There is not one penny charge; the articles in the newspaper, magazines, radio show presentations, and television shows are all free, and all you need is the ability, persistence, and confidence to keep trying until you obtain this important exposure. Too often catalog owners think the only way to get promotion is to pay for it, but public relations can be your strategy to make your business more profitable.

Consider your target market

Let people know what type of catalog you produce, what product and services make your catalog one of the best in the field. A local newspaper article will not hurt your public relations program, but if your market is future brides for your catalog on brides, you will only reach the future brides in your local area. Your public relations program must be planned and focused sharply on your target market, and, once combined with a marketing plan, your program acts as a double-edge sword to reach your target market. Chapter 16 will focus on marketing; this chapter will be devoted to public relations methods which will move you ahead of other competitors in your field.

Public relations means being at the right place at the right time. For example, I attended a book convention in New York and met an author who writes for a national tabloid, one with over 5 million circulation, who asked me about my book. I gave her a free copy of the book, and a few months later a full article was published on my book, my catalog, and my activities in the field. I would never have met this author without being at the show which brought together many people in the field. Be willing to appear where people or groups associate with a common purpose.

Another well-known catalog owner attended an environmental trade show; since his catalog stresses use of products which are friendly to the environment, he found many new customers and possible suppliers for the catalog marketing business. Your catalog has a target market, and your public relations campaign can stress the uniqueness of your products and why customers should buy from you.

Public relations has to do with courting the best suppliers and asking what special terms you can obtain from them. This involves more than simply asking for the normal terms when you buy from your suppliers. Lillian Katz, the founder of Lillian Vernon, the famous catalog marketing company, will ask her suppliers for exclusive rights for their products. Exclusive rights means the supplier will not sell to mail order people or retail outlets. When Lillian cannot get exclusive rights, she then asks for short-term exclusive rights, 60, 90, 120 days; another option is simple mail order rights. You cannot get special terms unless you ask for them.

Use news releases

The news release is your best public relations tool. The news release, also called a "press release," is one of the best ways to get free advertising for your business. The news release is a news statement about your firm, new staff, new services, exclusive rights, recent appearances at a convention, speeches you have made recently, publications such as articles or books you or your staff have written, awards received, donations you recently made to the local library, homeless shelter, or church. A news release which is professionally prepared and sent to the correct person at the newspaper, radio station, magazine, or television show will have a good chance to get printed or used.

Why do media outlets use news releases? Many newspapers, magazines and radio and television stations are always looking for information about interesting things going on in the area or in a special interest area. The news release is geared to present a subject in a clear, concise manner, and, when it is interesting to read, the editor will use it.

A news release is an $8\frac{1}{2} \times 11$" sheet of paper, usually white, but it can be another color, such as yellow, with double-spaced type to permit the editor to edit it, and it is filled with facts and news about your business. For example, if the news release is about your new catalog, tell why you started the catalog, what target market you selected, and what products and services you will sell. Notice I said facts and news—not advertising terms such as how your catalog is the best, how it will beat the competition, and why the prices are the lowest in the field. Save these important principles for your advertising and marketing campaign; don't hinder your news release by including these in your free news release. When your news release crosses the line and becomes a selfish advertisement, the editor will simply throw it in the waste basket. Focus on the facts and news and try to educate the public and your target market on what you have to offer them. Once your news release connects, you will get orders and important exposure which is important to your business. A sample news release is shown in Fig. 14-1.

How long should the news release be?

The best length is 1 page; many editors will edit length, printing only the amount they feel is needed in their publication. Write out the news release in rough form first, and then read it over; cut out any extra words, jargon, or unneeded phrases. A good news release should have a good headline, an introduction, body, and summary. Keep writing until you get a news release which communicates your message fully. Proofread it to remove

William J. Bond
President, Best Business Books
67 Melrose Ave.
Haverhill, MA 01830
(508) 858-6791

News Release

For release this Spring, the publication date of William J. Bond's book, *199 Time-Waster Situations and How to Avoid Them.*

A new book is now available to help people manage their most important resources: *time.*

How often have you heard teachers, engineers, salespeople, food service managers, administrators, retailers, accountants, writers, computer workers, investment specialists, insurance representatives, politicians, customer service specialists claim they could do their job better if they had more time? Everyone has the same amount of time each day, and this book will show you how to use it. *199 Time-Waster Situations and How to Avoid Them* will appeal to everyone and is a timely book for the 1990s. The people who can use their time to get the important work done, and get around the major time-waster situations, will keep their jobs and get the opportunities for promotion.

Time-waster situations are all around you, from procrastination, people, machines, methods, communications, overmanaging, planning, proper balance, and orientation toward action. This new book fully describes the situation and develops a practical yet workable way to get around it.

William J. Bond is the author of this new time management book. Bond has been writing for over 20 years on time management and has developed time management seminars for professionals in all fields; he is a popular dynamic teacher in college programs. Bond has appeared on many radio and television shows, most recently on the national *Smart Money* television show on CNBC. Bond uses his time management principles in his life—he has three full-time professions, professor, writer, and consultant, and still has time for his wife and two children. Bond says, "Time is everything, it is your life. I dedicated the book to those who use their most important resource: *Time.*"

To order copies of this book, ask for it at your local bookstore or you may order it by phoning free: 1-800-771-FELL. The book will be featured in the *Best Books Spring Catalog.*

Figure 14-1. News release. Your news release can be one of your most important public relations tools. Include facts about your catalog and your products and services, rather than citing the benefits of your products and services versus your competitors' products and services. One news release published is worth the value of a full-page advertisement.

incorrect spellings. Get it typed professionally, or use your own word processor, and print up at least 100 to 200 copies.

Send the news release to your target market

Hit your target market directly by sending the news release to newsletter editors in your field. For example, I sent my news release to newsletters in the business field; a number of newsletters mentioned my catalog in their heavily read publications, and I received orders right away. Mail out your newsletters immediately when your catalog is brand new, when your new product line is introduced, when you first received your award. Strike when you have a news-related feature for your target market. Some catalog owners personally deliver their news release. Once you mail out your news release, don't call the editors to find out their decision; they are too busy, and once you irritate them it might hurt you with future releases. Enclose a glossy photograph when discussing new products. Watch future issues of the publication to see whether they used your release. Only a few of the hundreds of news releases which are received weekly are used. Never get discouraged; remember, you cannot get the promotion until you prepare and send it out.

Find new public relations ideas

Just because company A is using a certain technique does not mean you must also try this technique in your public relations program. Try something not used by any other catalog owner or business owner in your area or in your general catalog field. Be willing to try something so unique it might fail: At least you have tried to be creative, and the people who succeed in this creative manner will become leaders in this business. For example, one catalog owner in Maryland set up some of her products at an elementary school fair in her area, and decided to donate 30 percent of the total proceeds to help the school build a much needed gymnasium. The local paper sent a staff writer to cover the story, and a huge article appeared in the paper; the trade magazine also had an article on this unique donation by a catalog owner. You can do the same. Donate a percentage of your proceeds at your next trade show, for example, to a worthy cause. Look at your products or services in a different way and then decide on how you can keep your name and products in the public eye.

Start a customer newsletter

A catalog marketing owner in Nebraska decided to keep customers on his house list interested in his new products by sending out a customer newsletter in between his spring and fall catalog editions. The newsletter describes the new products, why these products were selected, and how they can benefit the regular customers. The newsletter is now offered free, but the response has been so good on the newsletter that the owner may charge for subscriptions soon. If you are an expert on a particular subject or feel you're so interested in a particular subject with a specific target market, the newsletter business might be for you. My new book, *Home-Based Newsletter Publishing: A Success Guide for Entrepreneurs,* published by McGraw-Hill, can be ordered by calling 800-262-4729, or ask for it at your favorite bookstore. Your own newsletter can be an important extension to your catalog marketing business, and you can make excellent money and at the same time earn the recognition of your peers. Many opportunities present themselves for radio and television appearances and even interviews on the telephone for people who publish their own newsletters. The real benefit of your own newsletter is the exposure to many people, groups, and associations which will look to you as a specialist, speaker at a future meeting, and even a consultant. You are selling your expert knowledge and advice. One newsletter in New Hampshire is geared toward people in the consulting field, and each issue includes books, manuals, and supplies used by the subscribers. A catalog owner from California specializing in pet supplies started a customer newsletter that was in such demand that he hired a freelance writer to write the monthly newsletter; the catalog owner is happy with the prestige and the extra money. You might consider this same idea.

Get your name out in the media

The easiest way to become known and fully recognized as an expert in a field is to appear in a trade or national magazine. Getting an article published in your trade magazine is impressive public relations at a much higher level than advertising your products or services in a full-page advertisement in the same magazine. The article is important because it proves the publisher and the magazine editor agreed this article is timely and relevant to the subscribers, and without the subscribers they have no business. The article is your medium to communicate your grasp of the field, or it may simply help the readers solve a problem in their field. The article becomes your business card because it will give your name, your catalog's name, the name of your business, and its address and telephone number. People will be able to get in touch with you. A catalog owner from Nevada makes copies of her articles and sends them out to her customers or sales leads. Many new catalog sales have been developed because of the publication of those important articles. When they are sent out, each article is personally autographed such as below.

To: Sally Bradford, Purchasing Agent

Best of Luck, enjoy my recent article.

Jessica Tallman,

Catalog Owner/Author

Remember, most editors have never experienced what you have learned in selecting products, services, and printing of your own catalog, so you can share this important merchandising knowledge. Your message is very important; since it needs to be written you can do it, just try.

Business cards are essential

The small cost of printing up to 1000 copies of business cards is a small price compared to the excellent sales opportunities these cards give you. The business card should include your name, title of your catalog, and the name of some of the key products or services you sell in your catalog. The key benefit of business cards is the ability to educate people about what you sell. Include your business card in letters to suppliers, other catalog houses, letters to people in the trade, and customers. Keep business cards in your possession at all times; if you're on the road, keep some extra cards in your automobile. Some catalog owners keep them in their wallets or purses so they are handy to present to others. One owner of a national catalog from Illinois encloses a copy of his business card when he sends a letter to an unhappy customer.

It tells the customer, Please call me directly if you experience any further problems. This same owner is willing to give his home telephone number to his customers.

Talk about your catalog subject in a seminar

People want to know about you and your products, so why not set up a seminar at the local business college, technical school, or community school or community college in your area? The seminar can be as short as 1 hour or as long as 4 to 6 hours. You can talk about your catalog subject field; for example, one catalog owner selling exercise and running equipment set up a seminar to show how the equipment and a planned exercise program could help people of all ages. At the end of the seminar free catalogs were handed out along with a $5-off coupon on any purchase made over $25. The seminar gives you an opportunity to meet people directly who are part of your target market and who can give you their opinion of your products and services. The seminar attendees will also tell other people about your seminar and your products and services. This word-of-mouth advertising is essential to build your business. It can generate 10 to 20 percent of your sales, depending on your products and services. Once you run a successful seminar, others can be scheduled to run weeks or months into the future.

Sell your products to companies for incentives or prizes

Say a toy manufacturer wants to increase the sales to dealers and independent stores; the manufacturer gives points for each product sold, so that once a dealer gets at least 500 points the dealer can choose a free gift from your gift catalog. This is an excellent opportunity to build your sales, increase your house list, expand your products to a new market, and continue shipping your products on a regular basis. Your product is taken home and shown to others, and your sales are increased. The important consideration in accepting an agreement with a company to sell for prizes is the cost of the administration of the program, counting points, evaluating, and shipping. Make sure your agreement with the company is in writing and is reviewed by your attorney, and make it for 30 to 60 days in the beginning, so you can make a change if this is not in the best interest for your catalog house.

Give talks at trade associations, clubs, and schools

Florence Holmes is the owner of a gift catalog in Delaware, and she was recently invited to speak about her business at a trade association meeting in Virginia. Florence was nervous when she was originally booked for the talk, but once she determined she would talk about her business and the experience she gained from her business, she got down to business, and finished the outline for her talk. The talk went very well. Florence gave out many of her catalogs, and she handed out a number of her business cards to people who were interested in buying or discussing drop-shipping arrangements. Always take advantage of every speaking opportunity, because it can turn out to be a sales opportunity to sell more products or services. I recently accepted an invitation to speak to a high school group about my business and how I got interested in the catalog business; I showed my products and gave them some advice for getting into the catalog marketing field. At the end of my talk I handed out my literature and catalogs so the group could take them home to place their orders.

Donate your product to a worthy cause

The Boston public-sponsored television station has a telethon show to raise money for the station and auctions off products and services donated by the business community. Donate one of your lead products to such a show, providing that the station mentions your name, catalog name, and how to get additional catalogs from you. This public relations cannot be purchased from a full-page advertisement in a magazine—this is direct to television viewers from all over the region or country. I received the news article shown in Fig. 14-2 for a book I donated to my library as a gift.

Tap the television market for free

You can get excellent exposure to the target market by television. Many stations today have subject areas which will match your target market for your catalog. Before you try to book an appearance on a television talk show, why not try to start your own cable show in your area or try to get booked on a local cable show? By appearing on a local cable show, you get the experience of talking to television viewers in your area, and you get a better understanding of the television show process. Once you get the local experience, you can select talk programs targeting

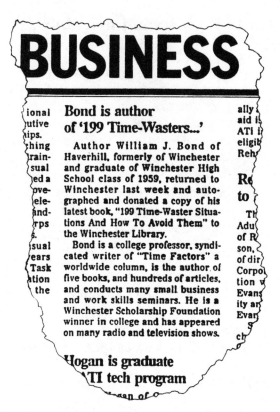

Figure 14-2. Business news clipping. A news release to your local or regional newspapers or to your trade magazine can offer you excellent public relations opportunities, even when you donate your products and services.

your market, and then present yourself to them. Giving the local cable station as a reference is an excellent first step to getting booked on a show. Remember, be willing to share your information with the audience, make your presentation entertaining, and show your enthusiasm. For example, I appeared on my local cable show, in the beginning of my catalog marketing career, but I then applied to other larger shows, and appeared on a national show, CNBC's the *Smart Money* television show, with viewers and callers from all over the country.

Radio stations have millions of listeners

Radio and television shows live or die—stay on the air or leave—based on their ratings. Their ratings also have a direct effect on the amount and quality of advertisers who pay for their radio or television commercials. When a radio show program manager, the person in charge of selecting guests for a show, makes the final decision to book a guest for a show, the important consideration is whether or not the guest will help the ratings for the show. I started with small radio stations, and then booked larger and larger stations, but the first booking is always the most difficult one to obtain.

Let's say your catalog offers gift items for men. Call the station during off-programming hours; if the show is on from 2 to 4 p.m., call in the morning, introduce yourself, get the programming manager's full name and address, and tell why you feel you should appear on their radio show. Stress the benefits of the listeners to your appearance; for example, show how you can inform the listeners about choosing the best gifts for men, what men look for in a gift, what the most popular gift in your catalog is, how you pick your products, how people can surprise the man in their lives with a special gift. Notice that your appearance is well thought out, and its main mission is to entertain, to inform the radio audience.

When you talk to the program manager the first time, offer to follow up with sending more information about you, your catalog, and your business. Then send a letter thanking the programming manager for his or her time and give a list of 10 different benefits your appearance would offer the audience. Tell the program manager you would get back by telephone in about a week. Send a glossy photograph of at least two of your most popular products and enclose a recent catalog and your business card. In a week's time, providing you didn't hear from the program manager, call the station again and ask for the booking. I will usually say, "I have my appointment book out right now, and Wednesday afternoon on the 12th at 2 p.m. is fine for me. Will that time meet with your approval?" Now wait for the answer. If the answer is yes, you have a booking; if it's no, you need to find out why. Listen to any objections, and then reiterate all the benefits you could offer the audience, and, if this type of show has not been done in the recent past, mention this in your closing statement. Even if the answer is still no, continue to call on a monthly basis until you get booked on the show.

The competition is strong to get on radio shows, so expect some resistance in the beginning. Once you get booked on the show, write a thank-you letter to the programming manager and make certain that you show up the day of the booking, on time, ready to do the best possible job. Once you do a good job on

the show, repeat bookings are much easier to obtain. One catalog owner from Maryland gives his name and telephone number
to radio and television shows in the Maryland area, with his permission to call him when a guest cannot make an appearance.
He readjusts his schedule to get to the radio or television show
to be a substitute guest. You can do the same.

Build your media network

As you begin to appear in radio, television, and print, you learn
the names and major players who make the decisions on what
guests are booked and what articles are published. Be loyal to
the radio station that booked you in the first place. Don't jeopar-
dize this trust by booking at the same time with a rival radio
show in the same city. When you do this once, you will find
future bookings very difficult to obtain. Program managers follow
other shows and their guests very closely; once you find a show
willing to book you, show your gratification by being loyal. Later
when you are doing something new, let the station know about
it, and ask for a rebooking.

Use good phone skills

Public relations begin and end with good on-the-phone manners.
When a customer or prospect calls you on the telephone, how
you handle the call and how you give individual attention to the
needs of the caller can make the difference between an order or
no order, the difference between success and failure. Let's listen
to a call right now—you're Jennifer Samuels of the New Image
Catalog Company.

> YOU: Good morning, this is Jennifer Samuels of New Image
> Catalog.
>
> CALLER: I received the catalog today. I'm Greg Smith. Do you
> have a guarantee with the Dual Time Clock, product
> N3240?
>
> YOU: Yes, everything is fully guaranteed, Mr. Smith.
>
> CALLER: Thank you. Do you have the pigskin backpack in
> suede color?
>
> YOU: Let me see, yes, we do have it in suede, Mr. Smith.
>
> CALLER: Thank you for your help.

You: Many thanks for your call, Mr. Smith, can I take your order right now? We will ship it today.

Caller: Yes, here is my order.

Notice what happened here. The catalog owner was polite, made the caller feel he was very important, gave all the information quickly and accurately, and wound the call up thanking the prospect by asking for, and obtaining, the order. Studies show than when a prospect thinks enough about your product or service to call with questions, you have a better possibility of getting the sale. Listen to your employees talking to your prospects and customers—this is the most important communication in any catalog marketing company. Give training in customer service when you find your company needs it.

Call talk programs. Some catalog owners regularly call nationwide talk programs and discuss their new products and services; the listeners get to know you as a regular caller, and the host will sometimes ask your address so the listeners can request a catalog. I call a radio station that goes to 39 states on a regular basis—WBZ Radio in Boston.

Summary

Public relations is important to help you build your image and inform and educate your target market and public in general on your products and services. The news release is the most important tool in the public relations field—use it regularly. Start a customer newsletter. Write a trade magazine article. Print up 1000 business cards. Run your own trade show or seminar. Give talks at your trade groups or conventions. Tell people about your business—people forget, so remind them of your product or service. Donate something in your catalog for publicity. Get on radio and television shows. Sell yourself to get the bookings. Build your media network. Public relations means good phone manners. Call a talk program—become a regular caller. Now let's discuss testing your catalog market next.

15

Testing

The one major benefit of the catalog or direct mail business is the ability to test everything in the business, including products, prices, advertisements, lists, postal classes, offers, and copy approaches. The new rule in testing is to test only essential things; for example, testing the color of your reply envelope or order form is not as important as testing the relationship of price on the sales of product A. Test that which can help you earn more profits or cut your cost. Profits are essential to keep your business growing. One way you can increase your profits by $1 is to increase your sales by $1, and the other way to increase profits is to cut costs by $1. With the advent of personal computers more information can be generated at lower cost, and you need to use this information in the decision-making process in your business. Take the time to do the test, but, more important, use this information to make your company and catalog better.

Product testing

Once you select a product or service for your catalog, how do you determine whether you should continue to run it? Keeping a catalog profitable means you have products and services which make a profit for you mailing after mailing, sale after sale. You send products by way of your catalog to people all over the country and the world; in order for each product or service to pay for this long trip it must be able to sell itself over and over. Test the sales for each product regularly and determine if the product is pulling its weight by offering to the business regular profits. You must support your products by offering as much service as possible to your consumers; the more services you offer, the more the consumers will support your business. Keep testing any additional services, and, when you find sales begin to increase, you can keep this service. Your prospects and customers enjoy a company willing to give them services to make it easier to buy. For example, Fred sells to industrial buyers with his industrial tool catalog; when sales started to drop, Fred decided to include an 800 number to call in orders. The sales began to increase. Test your services, and when they work, put them into full operation. In 1973 Joe Sugarman, catalog marketing owner of JS&A, who offers the *Products Which Think* catalog, decided he would try to give his prospects and customers an extra service: he would offer them a toll-free 800 number to order products after reading his catalog. The hesitation in the beginning was replaced by joy and satisfaction when the sales increased with the toll-free telephone service. This was a double win—a win for the prospects because they could use their credit cards and get a free call, and a win for the owner who sold more products and services.

Testing helps you to look at your performance and information to make the necessary changes. You learn from your failures. You learn how to make the necessary changes in order to get on the right track. For example, you selected a mailing list from the ABC company, and once you did the mailing, it failed to generate the 0.0166 percent necessary to continue to mail this rental list. Below you will find an analysis of the results from mailing some sample rental lists.

Date	List name	Cost per 1000	Total rental	No. mailed	Percent of return	Average sale	No. of sales	Total sales
Feb.	ABC	$70	$350	5000	0.0130	$33	65	$2145
Feb.	TRC	60	300	5000	0.0170	36	85	3060

Since the ABC list is not pulling sales above the 0.0166 percent, you might want to explore other lists which have the potential to give you long-term profits for your business. Always do a sample mailing to determine if the list works; once you determine it works for your catalog, you are now free to go to larger rentals of the same list. Continue to evaluate your list rentals and their performance for your catalogs.

Test the sales performance of your products

You will succeed in your catalog marketing business by selecting the best possible products, which means you evaluate your suppliers and then present your product and services to look the very best possible. You tried to become an expert in the product or service, and you asked some people knowledgeable in the field about the product as well. You carefully screened the suppliers, so you could get the products at the best possible price and on the best terms possible. Monthly you want to evaluate your products or services and their ability to sell in your catalog. Don't compare the sales numbers the supplier gives you for the product; evaluate it from the sales from your catalog or advertisements. Below you will find a test on products evaluated against one another for sales:

Date	Product	No. of sales	Price	Amount of sales	Sales rank of products
March	A	100	$45	$4500	1
March	B	70	40	2800	2
March	C	25	50	1250	4
March	D	55	39	2145	3

Every six months you should consolidate these monthly tests to determine your winners, losers, and marginal products. Cut the products which are not making a profit for you, and move the highest-selling products toward the front of your catalog. Some catalog owners try to put together a mini-catalog with just the best-selling products, and they mail it to the house list or the names on the house list called heavy users because these people continually buy products month after month.

Test your advertisements

To increase your sales and your house list you should continually run small-space advertisements in specific magazines offering your lead products and your catalog to the prospects. Inquiries are not enough; you need to turn these prospects into buyers. To avoid spending excessive money on advertisements which fail to work or having excessive inquirees who fail to buy, test your advertisements regularly. The following is a test of your advertisements:

Date	Advertise-ment	Magazine	Type	Cost	No. of inquiries	Percent converted to sales	Total sales
Feb.	A	*Popular Mech.*	Classified	$100	200	10	20
Feb.	B	*Changing Times*	Small-space	150	150	6	9
March	C	*Income Opport.*	Classified	125	115	11	13

You paid less for your classified advertisements, and you earned more sales, 10 for advertisement A, and 11 for advertisement C; advertisement B, the highest-priced one, only turned in 9 sales for you. Evaluate both the quality of your advertisement as well as its placement in your magazine for a period of 3 to 6 months before you make a decision on moving the advertisement to another magazine.

Test for the best month to mail

Many catalog marketing owners find that the very best month is January for them. Other owners selling Christmas season gifts must get their catalogs in the mail by late September to obtain the maximum sales. I recommend that during your first year in the business you print up enough catalogs to send out a mailing at least once a month to your house list, your rental list, and the inquiries you received from your small-space advertisements. Below you will find a test of month-by-month sales, including the average sales and total sales for the catalog owner, in the first year of the business:

Sales by Month

Month	Amount of sales	Average sale	Total sales
Jan.	100	$40	4000
Feb.	108	42	4536
March	103	39	4017
April	90	37	3330
May	85	35	2975
June	95	38	3610
July	70	32	2240
Aug.	75	36	2700
Sept.	83	41	3403
Oct.	110	39	4290
Nov.	123	44	5412
Dec.	128	46	5888

This catalog owner had strong months from October to March, and business sales dropped from April to August during the warmer time of year. Since catalogs have a long life, it might be a good idea to mail in late August or early September for the large fall mailing and February or March for the large spring mailing. To determine when the catalog was mailed, you can key the order form JA for January, DE for December, and so on. Each catalog and target market differs, so test closely to determine which is your busiest time of year and make certain you get your mailing out in sufficient time to get your sales.

Use accurate testing techniques

Consider using two-flight testing in your catalog business. When you find that a specific rental list of the ABC Company sold a percentage higher than the other two lists, try not to make a quick decision on mailing 50,000 catalogs using the list. Under the two-flight testing theory, do another test using the ABC Company list and two other rental lists before you make your final decision.

There are seasonal variations in mail order. Try to mail out all the pieces of your offer at the same time to get the most reliable test. Avoid sending out smaller quantities weekly; rather, send all 10,000 catalogs on the first day in the month and your mailing will be consistent to all prospects. Catalogs arriving just prior to a family holiday such as Christmas, Easter, Thanksgiving, and Independence Day will not get the readership and the initial reception that catalogs arriving on a non-holiday week do.

Make sure your test sample is large enough. Too often catalog owners try to establish an answer to a question without a large enough sample to justify it. For example, you mail 200 catalogs primarily to a section of the country experiencing high unemployment; when you find the results poor, the conclusion that the catalog did not do the selling job is erroneous. You must then go out and mail at least 2000 to 5000 catalogs to a national list which represents a good cross-section of your target market.

Test product returns regularly

You might make a sale but, in the catalog business, some customers will return the product or service and expect their money returned, a credit issued on their credit card if the purchase was made this way, or a credit to purchase other products. Returns are very complicated; sometimes a return is made because the product does not meet the needs of the buyer, the product is perceived as too expensive, or perhaps the product did not hold up to the demands or use by the customers. Find out the reason for the return at the time of the return or as promptly as possible. When you find product A is being returned at a higher rate than other products in your catalog, find out why. Is it the price? Is it the copy approach—are you overselling versus the value? Determine the reason and make the necessary changes.

Test different sections of your catalog

All successful catalogs have products grouped according to the type of product and the needs and interests of the target market. For example, one gift catalog owner has gifts for the home, for children, for special holidays and occasions, and jewelry. Do a test periodically to see how each section is doing for a six-month or one-year basis. See Fig. 15-1 for a graph that shows which section is selling the most gifts and which section is falling behind. When you determine a section such as the children's gift section is not keeping up, you might want to review your products

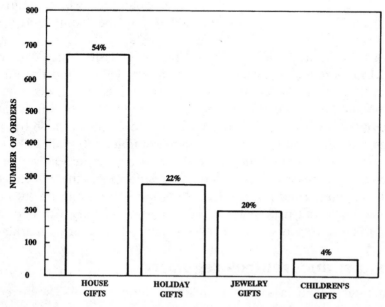

Figure 15-1. Sales on sections of your catalog. Keep a record of what sections of your catalog sell the most products or services. Review the copy in the sections that are selling well. Make the necessary changes in sections selling poorly.

closely, check the copy approach, and take another look at the prices to determine why your target market does not see your catalog as the place to purchase gifts for their children. Perhaps your target market is using another catalog, specifically geared to selling children's gifts, and it is getting a larger share of the market.

When you do this test you readily see it might be a better idea to focus more of your energy into building up the jewelry or holiday gift section rather than try to get the children's gift section selling to a level competitive with the other sections. You want to introduce your reader to exciting products in the beginning of your catalog. When you decide to terminate the section for children's gifts, you are not obligated to purchase and store these products any longer; you can put all your focus on the other sections. Just as a retailer does a sales test on each department and treats each department as a separate entity, you must do so with the different sections of your catalog. Know what your target market wants, and test for what products or services these customers are buying from you.

Test the theme of your catalog

Each catalog should focus on a theme to get the prospect into a particular mindset and then present the products and services which reinforce this specific theme. For example, a national catalog owner selling sporting equipment, exercise equipment, and office equipment is using a theme of quality products with affordable prices. The owner makes it a point to position each product in use, so the prospect can see how the product can be used in his or her lifestyle. Do a test like the following on your themes to determine which theme connects to your target market to sell the most per product or service:

Date	Theme	No. of sales
Spring	Saving the energy	1000
Fall	Start your business	1100
Spring	Twenty-first-century products	1150
Fall	Holiday bargains	1310

Your themes are essential to keep your prospects and customers buying, and once you find a theme which works, such as the twenty-first-century products theme, you can continue with this theme in future catalog issues. For example, you could have two themes working together, the twenty-first-century products as well as a quality products theme, while you work hard to deliver the best products all over the country and the world for your target market. Some catalog owners key their order forms to determine what theme was used to get that order; for example, s/engy would be the key for spring/energy, and f/hb stands for fall/holiday bargains. When you find a theme which works, stay with it as a co-theme. Your catalog theme must be a creative thread, which is weaved from the front cover to the back cover; it cannot be placed on the front cover without having the copy and presentation all the way through.

Make your tests uniform

Let's say you want to test two copy approaches in your catalog; rather than spend the high price of doing two different catalogs with completely different copy, try to change two pages on the catalog. Look at the example below showing catalog A, using the copy approach using emotional words, and then catalog B, using a more rational approach: how you can save money and get a better value for your money.

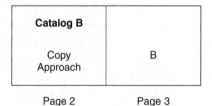

Catalog A			Catalog B	
Copy Approach	A		Copy Approach	B
Page 2	Page 3		Page 2	Page 3

When you mail your catalogs out to your list, keep your test uniform by mailing out by 1, 2, 1, 2, 1, 2, 1, 2, 1, 2, 1, 2—catalog A goes to every other one, rather than your sending all A catalogs to the first half of your list, which might include just the east coast of the United States, and sending B catalogs to the last part of your list, which might include just the western part of the country.

Testing is a process you can learn

Focus on the prompt testing of important aspects of your business to help you earn more profits in your business. One catalog owner, who has been in the business for over 20 years, uses four important words or phrases to help her get the best possible information for her testing activities. The words include *what, when, where,* and *to what extent. What* is to help you focus on just what you want to test: the copy, the price, the list, or the sales of the products. *When* can help you determine when something happens in your business, whether it be just sometimes, often, or all the time. *Where* helps you to understand whether something only happens with certain customers, certain products, or certain regions of the country. *To what extent* helps you to determine whether something happens to just a small portion of your products or to all of them, to some of your prospects or to all of them. Using these four basic words and phrases will help you to describe the symptoms of a problem.

Some catalog owners look at testing as an opportunity to make their catalog marketing business better. You can stay competitive when you continue to make changes to keep up to date and prove to your prospects and customers you care about quality and their full satisfaction. Below is a listing one major catalog owner uses based on five steps to make improvements in his business:

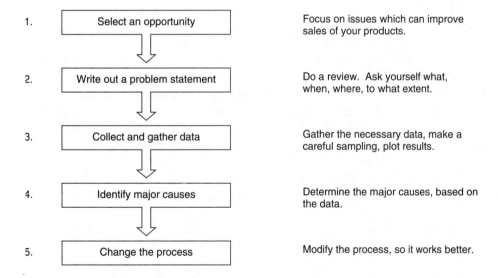

1. Select an opportunity — Focus on issues which can improve sales of your products.

2. Write out a problem statement — Do a review. Ask yourself what, when, where, to what extent.

3. Collect and gather data — Gather the necessary data, make a careful sampling, plot results.

4. Identify major causes — Determine the major causes, based on the data.

5. Change the process — Modify the process, so it works better.

Testing is time consuming, it's costly, and it can be frustrating for catalog owners who would like to be doing other things in their business. Testing can be the difference between success and failure, and a profit or a loss, the difference between a business you will sell someday for a substantial amount of money, or one you will just hand over to someone at a nominal price. Testing is a tool to help you put your business in the best working order to keep selling, day after day, week after week, year after year.

Keep a bible on your testing results

Testing is difficult and time consuming but essential to save money and increase your sales and profits. When you complete a test, write up a summary of it and include it in your test results log for further use. Read it over often and use the information regularly. For example, when you determine that an advertisement in magazine A failed miserably when you charged $2 for the catalog, keep this in mind in future insertions to this magazine. Rather than depend on your memory, use the information in your test results log to make decisions. Another important consideration is your copy approach: compare how your sales are affected by the factual copy approach versus an emotional copy approach for a specific target market. Refer to your testing log for these results.

Summary

Making improvements in your business is not just sheer guesswork, it takes a discipline and the courage to face reality by doing testing of the important elements in your catalog business. Test your products before you put them into your catalog, and, once the catalogs are printed, keep testing them for stability. Testing gives you a performance rating and the data to make the changes for success. Test your advertisements and lists. Test the best time to sell your products. Do a two-flight test to save time and effort. Look for seasonal variations. Make the test sample large enough. Why did you get a large return on product A? Test different sections of your product catalog. Themes should be tested regularly. Make your test as uniform as possible. Testing is a process you can learn to improve yourself and your business. Refer to your testing results log regularly.

16

Marketing opportunities for the twenty-first century

Nothing is constant but change: Your business is always changing, and you must continue to review all marketing opportunities available to you to keep your prospects and customers buying. To succeed, your business must get sales orders, and to do this will require persistent mailings and following up on inquiries so that people can buy from you. They key is to get your catalog to the people who have the most interest in your product right now and then follow up with other opportunities until they buy from you.

Use two-step marketing

Successful marketing in the catalog business means dealing directly to your target market, and one of the best ways to do this is to use the two-step marketing system. This system means you advertise one of your lead products in a magazine especially geared to your product and ask for the inquirees to write for additional information. Once you receive an inquiry, you then send out information and your catalog, and let the prospect make the buying decision. Depending on the quality of the inquiries from the magazine, you could get up to 10 to 15 percent response to your catalog offer. You are then also building up your house list in the process.

I used the two-step marketing process in the beginning of my business selling business manuals, by using the classified advertisements and then following it up with additional sales material to get the order. My first advertisement received 80 responses, and out of this I received enough orders to pay for another classified advertisement in another magazine. I did this for a number of months and built my house list to 3000 names. During the next few years, running advertisements and continuing the two-step marketing method, I built my house mailing list to over 30,000 names. These names are from all over the country from Maine to California. All these names have received my catalog to purchase additional information. A sample classified advertisement is shown below which could run in a national men's magazine.

> **FREE**
> New catalog on Antique Clocks.
> Many unique, one of a kind clocks.
> Write: Clocks Catalogue, 100 Main
> St., Winterlong, MA 01830.

Any inquiry you receive informs you that the respondent is interested enough to write to you about your ad. Now you have the challenge to turn this inquiree into a full-fledged customer and keep her or him buying for life. Make an inquiry card right away so you can trace the marketing activities you use to keep selling the inquiree.

Marketing success requires a budget

Many catalog owners find that getting the catalog prepared and printed is a real challenge, and then they fall into the temptation of relaxing rather than moving into the marketing stage to make the business work. Marketing means using a set of activities to present your catalog products and services to your target market. On the next page you will find a list of the most essential activities to turn out sales for your business for the first six months of your business.

Budget for Marketing

Catalog preparation	$———————
Catalog printing	———————
Postage mailing	———————
Advertisements	———————
News releases	———————
Business cards, stationery	———————
Telephone, answering service, and/or fax	———————
Association membership	———————
Total	$———————

Once you get a total for your budget, divide this by 6, and you will have the total cost to run your business each month for the first 6 months. Your goal will be to work hard enough to generate enough sales and profits to fund your business for the next 6 months. Marketing is your fuel to keep your business running. Sales make your business succeed, so continue to focus your energy on sales.

How do you find the best magazines?

Look over the current magazines in your home or office right now, and review the classified or small-space advertisements shown in them. Review the demographics and psychographics discussed in an earlier chapter in the book. What type of magazines does your target market read? Ask the reference librarian at your local or regional library to give you a list of magazines which reach the people in your target market area. For example, people who like to fix their own automobiles read *Popular Mechanics,* writers read *Writers' Digest* or *The Writer,* boat owners read *Yachting,* and people who want to keep up with the changes in our society and business read *Changing Times.* You can write to magazines and ask for their media kits, which are a listing of the total circulation and demographics, lifestyle, and content of the magazine. Look carefully at the paid circulation of the magazine—this means the people who paid their own money for the privilege of receiving the magazine during the next 12 months. Some advertisers confuse the paid circulation, let's say it is given at 200,000 people, to the pass-along circulation of 400,000. This pass-along circulation is merely an estimate of how many people read it, including the paid readers plus others. For example, the wife, a subscriber, reads the magazine and then passes it along to the husband to read. The paid readership has a vested interest in the magazine and will read it with more concentration, examine advertisements more, and generally give it more attention. The pass-along readership may buy, but it will be a harder sell to get this group to respond. The key for you is the paid circulation.

Market in special geographical areas

A catalog marketer selling services rented a mailing list of *Business Week* subscribers from New Hampshire and received a 4 percent sales response from it. A catalog owner from Connecticut selling sewing kits used a mailing list of people living in U.S. rural areas, and it turned out to be a very profitable mailing when it was sent just before the Christmas season.

Review your product or service carefully and determine where it would find the most likely buyers, and then do whatever is necessary to deliver your offer to them. Success in catalog marketing is being willing to fail "forward"—to keep trying until you find the most willing market for your catalog offers.

Get potential customers ready

One catalog marketer from California sends out a postcard to his potential customers and informs them that his 68-page catalog on computer supplies will be arriving at their homes within a few days. You might want to do a test on this strategy to see whether it will work for your catalog marketing program. Another catalog marketer offers a cover letter using a telegram format to get attention, and once the potential customer reads it, the message informs her or him that the catalog will be sent within a few days and describes the benefits of the products.

Good marketing means you take the time to educate others about what benefits your products and services offer your target market. Many companies spend millions of dollars in their advertising and marketing budget to inform and educate potential buyers.

Another strategy is to sell a booklet or report for $1 and send your catalog along for additional sales. During the past year I have offered a report, "200 Easy, Home-based Businesses," in a classified advertisement; once I receive the $1, which helps pay for the catalog and postage to send the report, I have found people who are very interested in my products and services. My report is worth much more than the $1 I request for it. I tie the report into the products in the catalog, so when my customer finishes the report, he or she will most logically move to the catalog and read it with more interest than if the catalog was sent alone. I also make it a point to tell the customer that she or he gets a $1 refund on the first sale, and this will give my customers another reason to fill out the order form or pick up the phone to call in the order. During the next month, this classified advertisement will appear in four national magazines:

BUSINESS OPPORTUNITIES
200 Easy Home-based Businesses Report and
Information Catalog, $1 (Refundable)
Professor Bond, 67W Melrose, Haverhill, MA 01830

Notice how I keyed the address so I can determine where the responses come from: The 67W stands for *Writers' Digest,* located in Cincinnati, Ohio, 67M represents *Money Making Magazine* based in Studio City, California, which has been around for many years. By offering the special report I am getting people to respond other than the people who simply want a free catalog and are sending a request to many catalog marketers at the same time. Once you send out to the free catalog requester, you might be competing with 8 to 10 other competitors.

When the results of the four magazines finally arrive, I will do a report similar to the one below showing classified advertising results to see which advertisements worked for me. Give yourself time to let your advertisement age; some people will not respond the first or second time they see your advertisement. Run it a number of times to get to see a trend. I recently spoke to the classified advertisement manager of *Writers' Digest,* Joan Bambeck; when asked about how long a catalog marketer should run a classified advertisement to make money, she replied, "All classified advertisers who really succeed run the same classified advertisement for 12 months." Many catalog marketers such as Melvin Powers, of Wilshire Books, the Mellinger Mail Order Company selling dealerships, run classified advertisements every month, year after year, to get maximum exposure for their products and services.

Date	Magazine	Cost	Sales	Profit on advertising
Jan.	*Changing Times*	$185	450	$265
Jan.	*Writers' Digest*	85	360	275

Consider running classified advertisements on a regular basis for special features such as reports, gifts, newsletters, or an incentive which would appeal to a target market for your catalog. Once you find a magazine which pulls good results, you can continue to run this advertisement until it stops working for you. The real value is the opportunity to get additional customers, and at the same time you get a chance to build your house list which was discussed earlier in the book. Your house list is important because it will offer you the opportunity to market your customers with greater flexibility in the future.

Power marketing is essential

The catalog marketers who survive in this competitive environment develop their own power marketing strategies to gain the special competitive edge over others in the field. *Power marketing* means you determine that your two most important roles are to continually create and keep customers. Doing this requires an ability to look at your product or service in a different way; look at the value to others—the benefits, the advantages, the attractive features—which will make your catalog universal in appeal and scope. Power marketing means getting and staying close to the customer and it means researching all the marketing techniques and strategies used successfully, starting with the manufacturers and dealers of the products and services you place in your catalog.

Far too often marketers try to reinvent the wheel by running advertisements, renting lists, and doing promotion which are previously researched and perfected by the manufacturer or dealer. Work with your manufacturer or vendor to advertise together and share with each other what is working for success. One catalog marketer called his vendor with a problem, excessive returns on a particular product; once they took the time to discuss the situation and then discussed common problems, the manufacturer talked about how her products were made, the costs, and safety precautions used to make them the best product possible. The catalog marketer soon realized that these important manufacturing advantages should be played up more in the catalog to increase sales and exposure to his products. This is the other side of power marketing: it is the curiosity of the engineer or scientist, always looking for special processes into marketing weapons to win the competitive condition. Power marketing means having the vision to bring your marketing strategies together with the public relations programs to give a one-two punch which will increase sales and word-of-mouth advertising for your catalog. Power marketing means using testimonials in a creative manner, to discuss not simply how a product performed but how the catalog owners responded to customers in need. The following is a sample testimonial using the power marketing principle:

> Thank you very much for sending out Amber Jones, your service engineer when your computer failed last month. When we purchased the computer from you by catalog, we wondered whether you could deliver the service and guarantee you promised. I am happy to report it is up and running now; we were able to finish up our end-of-year reports, thanks to Amber and your fine company.
>
> FRANK CONNELLY, PRESIDENT
> *Finest Computer and Software Company*

Power marketing is objective enough to look at the products and service from the side of the customer and not from the seller or the owner. Power marketing means sending out news releases on your new catalog, but it also means sending a complete news release which includes photographs of key products and services and following up to see what news releases were used and the reasons that they were used.

Power marketing means having a vision of what you want your company to do for your target market and then releasing all the resources within your company to reach this vision. It means taking all opportunities to showcase your catalog to others.

Power marketing means having trust in your customers and potential customers so you can start a revolution in your business area. Your vision and trust become a special magnet and foundation to build up larger and larger orders and opportunities for the future. As you begin your home-based catalog marketing business, I want you to evaluate your marketing strategies and marketing plan and then ask yourself whether you are fulfilling the principles we discussed in this chapter in a powerful way: power marketing. You have all the power in your hands; just use it.

What is the value of your customer?

Many first-time customers will begin with a small amount, just to try your product and your company. This first-time purchase is an extremely important challenge for you to make this new customer a steady customer and a customer for life. The total value of a customer is the amount of total sales of the company divided by the total customers you have obtained in the business. Below you will find the formula of the ABC Catalog Company for finding total value of their customers:

	Sales	Total customers	Average sales
ABC Company	$200,000	2000	$100

Total value of customer: $200,000 \div 2000 = $100

One way to increase the total value of your customer is to show how one product can benefit the customer and how products can be used with other products. This concept is illustrated by the catalog owner who tries to sell a fishing rod to the buyer, and, once the sale is made, then sells flies, tackle, fishing bags, rods, and other fishing equipment.

Some catalog owners will increase sales in their catalog by giving special offers, e.g., when you buy deluxe product A, you will get 20 percent off on product B. The packaging of your products can also help you sell by offering other products to the buyer. A message such as where to reorder when the product is used up also helps to increase your sales. One catalog marketer of office supplies tries to leave his name and address on each package so the buyer can buy the next product from him rather than buy it from a competitor.

Another important element to help your customers or potential customers buy from you is the consistency of your messages to them. For example, using the same name and address and logo, if you have one, on each piece of literature you send your customers, from the original catalog and order form to envelopes, letters, form letters, and any other correspondence, can leave a very favorable impression on the potential customer. You will have an advantage over other marketers who use various names and addresses and logos that confuse the potential customer. Stay consistent in giving your potential customers the best possible impression of you and what you sell. For example, if you are selling sporting goods, do everything possible to convey your speciality; if you are selling inspirational books, keep stressing your speciality in all your correspondence. Too often, catalog marketers just assume their customers know what they are selling; the marketers get sloppy about keeping a clear focus on their speciality, and the marketing vision gets blurred and sales go down. To increase the value of your customer, focus on what you do better than anyone else and keep doing it day after day, year after year.

Your success will be determined by your ability to increase this total value of the customers and implement strategies to replace with new customers the ones who will stop buying from you. Customers change their priorities, move, get ill, die, or change their interests. Your challenge will be to move your marketing and promotion strategies to attract new customers and keep them buying.

Marketing means solving problems and getting orders

Successful marketing in this environment and the future means having the ability to look at your business and try new ideas to capture all the benefits and advantages in your business. In your business you are a salesperson, and in selling you must be willing to tell the whole story, tell about how your product works and helped others and is a sound investment. Successful marketing by catalog is the result of hard work and an understanding of today's difficult-to-understand customers. You are a salesperson, whether you are willing to admit it or not. Good salespeople succeed in selling because they do things to help people buy. Nothing happens in any catalog business until a sale is made. You should consider the 21 principles below before choosing any product or service or writing the first word of copy for your catalog:

1. Know your product or service fully.
2. Keep up-to-date with competing products.
3. Set goals each day, and strive to reach them.
4. Listen to your potential customer.
5. Never wait for the product to sell itself; it needs your help.
6. Avoid making promises on delivery and prices which you cannot fulfill.
7. Offer a full guarantee to all your customers.
8. The first sale can be the beginning of a long relationship.
9. Your main job is to offer the best product or service possible to your prospects and customers.
10. Work harder to make yourself a better salesperson.
11. Keep aiming for the top.
12. Be curious about why people behave a certain way. Read books on human nature.

13. Be honest with others and yourself.

14. Believe in your product and offer.

15. Keep demonstrating your product creatively.

16. As a top salesperson, you build bridges from a product to a consumer.

17. Believe in your buyers.

18. You must stretch yourself into an even better salesperson each day.

19. You are a positive person and can see your own sales success.

20. You don't compare yourself to others but try to maximize on your potentials.

21. You watch your appearance and manners and act like you own success fully.

The way you feel about yourself and your product or service will have an important effect on the way you market and sell. Selling successfully is your most important principle, and it means completing the sale, not just creating interest and almost getting the sale. Successful catalog marketers know that almost everything is selling and then get to work to get it done.

Good marketing is a lifelong relationship with your customers

Keeping the customer buying requires the ability to deliver the best customer relations services possible. It means calling or writing to the customer when a question comes up, it means sending a check to customers when they overpay an order, it means doing the extra things to keep the customer satisfied and happy.

Not all catalog marketers can handle the customer service obligations, but they know how important it is for the customer in Nevada to get the correct size for his new shoes or for the woman in Maine who was sent the sweater with the wrong color to have it exchanged promptly. When you feel you cannot fulfill these customers' requests promptly, hire someone who will do it for you. Sometimes you can get a family member to do it; other times it can be someone willing to work a day or a half day a week to do these important duties for you.

As you start your business on a part-time basis, when customers call during the day, rather than have an answering machine take the message, you might think it a good idea to get someone such as a secretarial or business office to handle the calls for you. Having someone answer the phone records the information: who called, what is needed, how much is needed, telephone number, pricing and shipping considerations. Too often the message left on the answering machine is brief, and important information is not included. By having a live person answering your phone the customer can be asked, "Is there anything else we can send you today, Mrs. Jones? We have 10 percent off on all our doll's furniture this week, along with free shipping." Keep your relationship going strong by giving the best possible service in the business.

Create ideas to move beyond the competition

Sally Welch of Massachusetts, a successful marketer of seminars, reviews the sales of her business on a regular basis. When she finds that sales are not as high as they were for the same time last year, she will do an exercise called "brainstorming" to get new ideas to get the business back on track. Brainstorming is best when more than one person is doing it, and it includes a number of ideas listed on a blackboard or a sheet of paper; everything, even silly ideas, are included in the practice. Nothing, no matter how unusual, small, or large, is left out; all ideas are presented in the group. Below you will find some ideas which resulted from the brainstorming session at Sally's meeting:

Offer low-priced seminars.

Offer money-oriented seminars.

Offer home-based business seminars.

Offer free videotape.

Close seminars to certain groups.

Do national seminars.

Do regional seminars.

Do hour-long seminars.

Present 2½-hour seminars.

Don't do teachers.

Sell books at seminars.

Run 3- or 4-week seminars.

Go for *heavy users*.

Offer a mini-catalog on seminars.

Play games.

Spot difficult people in seminars.

Make difficult attendees into teachers.

Become a weekend school.

Offer certificate for each course.

Try a "How to Run Your Own Seminar" seminar.

Give test at end.

Guarantee all seminars.

Pay teachers a percentage.

Run three at a time.

Don't charge for registration.

Do weekend seminars.

Hire a commission promotion manager.

Promote on radio.

Try a "How to Challenge Your Assumptions" seminar.

Ask attendees what they want for courses.

Pay people to attend.

Place students when they complete a seminar.

Do videos—and sell them to people who can't attend.

Write.

Sell videos at end of course.

Try a "Survive Info Overload" seminar.

Do a "See the Big Picture" seminar.

From a brainstorming list, the group (or you) evaluates each idea, determining what are the best five or seven ideas for the group. These ideas can be used in the marketing strategies or ideas for your business. You can use this brainstorming technique for your catalog marketing business as well. Periodically review your sales per product or service and determine how you can increase the sales without spending additional money. Many ideas are available if you take the time to explore them. This technique can be used in many areas of your business as well, including solving problems such as choosing the best list, determining reason for high rates of returns for your products, researching low order amounts, and determining the best copy approaches for your business. Never say you cannot solve a problem until you have done a brainstorming session to uncover potential solutions or ideas.

Develop a sense of urgency

Successful marketing in the catalog business must produce a catalog which will motivate the reader to buy now rather than wait for another issue of your catalog or a competitor's catalog or simply to put buying off until later. The possibility of getting the customer to buy later is very small, so get the order while the iron is hot—the first time the reader reviews your catalog. In the auto business, the rule of thumb is to sell the customer the first time. When the customer turns to you and states, "I'm not ready right now—I'll be back soon," the chances for a return are remote, so try to keep the buyer in the showroom to complete the sale.

Marketing is selling what the customer wants to buy

Your product or service is made for the customer. Selling works when you listen closely to what the customer wants to buy and then take the necessary steps to deliver it. For example, Janice, a New Jersey children's clothing catalog owner, had an excellent beginning year in business. When the second year arrived, the original customers would not buy as large an order as the first one, and many were simply not buying. After calling some of her customers, Janice determined that many customers felt many of the same products of the original catalog were still on the second catalog, and they did not respond. Janice decided she would offer an additional service to motivate the people to buy, and she offered personalized sewing services, including monogramming, at a very small price. The sales began to increase, and now these services are a regular feature of the catalog. The personalized products became excellent gift items for birthdays and holidays.

Another example of personalizing your products is the catalog owner from California who writes manuals, books, and reports for small-business people. Since most of the publishing products are written by him personally, he offers to autograph each product purchased, to anyone the buyer selects, and will date the book as well. This is an example of doing autograph parties for your customers all over the country.

Place your catalog in directories

During the last two years I have received thousands of inquiries from people all over the country and from people in foreign countries for my free, yes free, listings in directories on catalogs. People enjoy receiving catalogs; many will purchase a directory at the local bookstore or store and then mail their requests for a copy of your catalog. The owners of these directories sometimes charge, but many times they give free listings to people who do catalog marketing. The only requirement is to fill out their directory listing application in full and send it back promptly. You will see your name in the directory in a number of months. The postcards and letters will appear shortly after the book appears on the shelves of the store.

A directory can also be a potential catalog product for you. Let's say your catalog offers products and services for consultants, and your mailing list is now getting more national in scope.

Consider putting together a directory listing for consultants by their speciality, for example, food business consultants, computer consultants, software consultants, government consultants, and marketing consultants. You can charge a fee for every person giving you a full listing, and it will pay for the printing of your directory. Let's say you charge $15 for a listing and you get 2000 consultants to sign up for the directory; you will receive $30,000 to print up your directory, and you can even sell your book to them at a reduced price, for, say, $2 off the regular $25 price of the directory. A directory is like a mailing list—it will age quickly and must be updated regularly or it will die of old age old with outdated, incorrect information.

Get as many directory listings as possible, but be careful; key your catalog order forms to determine who is ordering from you. For example, I use the letters *CC* to stand for *Catalog on Catalogs* directory and *TCD* to stand for *Toys Catalog Directory* to keep the sales per directory right up-to-date. Remember, although directory readers enjoy catalogs, they might not have as strong an interest in your products as the reader of a speciality magazine. This distinction between customers requires testing, which we discussed in the last chapter.

Try some new marketing techniques

Today simply mailing out a catalog to a rental list or even a house list may not be enough. You need to present your product in a different way to reach new people and increase your sales. One catalog marketer who sells personal-care products decided to start house parties, whereby he selects someone to give the party and invites friends and neighbors for the evening, usually on a weeknight, and the products are shown by the catalog owner and the host. A video is shown to the party guests to demonstrate how the products and services can be used in various lifestyles. Orders are taken after the video, refreshments are served, and catalogs are given to people who want to order later. The money is paid at the house party or is paid on delivery of the catalog to avoid billing the customer later. This is an excellent way to inform people of your business as well.

Another catalog market owner offers people, usually customers, the opportunity to have their friends and associates at work review and order from the catalog. Orders are taken at the office, and the seller then delivers to the buyer within a week. The money is paid directly to the seller, or sometimes credit is given, and the products can be paid for over an extended period. There is coordination and bookkeeping involved in this marketing technique, but as you can see there are many different ways to get people interested enough in your catalog to buy from you.

Build or swap for your best mailing list

Some catalog owners build their own list by swapping their list with another catalog owner or mail order owner. For example, I recently swapped 5000 of my inquirees' names for 5000 names from a catalog owner who offers consulting and business services. Since I felt there was not direct competition between us, I agreed to the mutual swap. When you make a swap for names, there is no money exchanged; you get to completely own the names, and you can mail to them as often as you determine is feasible. So that there is no problem after the swap transaction, I recommend that you and the other party sign the simple agreement, in a format shown below:

List Swapping Agreement

I, Amber Frederick of *Best Stars Catalog,* agree to swap 2000 of my customer names to the Nautical Catalog Company for 2000 of their names.

All names swapped can be mailed offers regularly and can be rented to other mailers in the future. There will be no charge or any money exchanged for the completion of the transaction or in the future.

Please sign and date in the space provided below:

_____   _____Date
Best Stars Catalog

_____   _____Date
Nautical Catalog Co.

Along with swapping lists, many catalog marketing owners build their own lists by compiling a list themselves. For example, let's say that you want to sell products to computer service people who specialize in personal computers; you could start your own list by taking names out of directories, phone books in your area, and phone books from all regions of the country. Many important lists can be compiled when you take the steps to obtain them systematically over a period of time. Some catalog marketers obtain names at trade shows, from trade associations, from chamber of commerce lists, and from service organizations. Many business opportunity organizations are listed in a directory sold over the counter at bookstores and news shops. Many catalog marketers who sell products and services for this market can compile a list for future mailings.

The key for compiling a list is to *test* the list often and continue to compile only when you find that the list is pulling enough sales for you to continue the time and effort involved in the compiling process. For example, after compiling 500 names for your new catalog, mail out to them and carefully record all sales for the mailing. Did you get any responses from your compiled list? Key your names which were compiled, so you can easily identify it. Below you will find a test which shows a mailing of a house list, compiled list, and a rented list.

Date	List	No. mailed	Percent of sales	Total orders
12/99	Compiled	2000	1	20
12/99	House list	2000	3	60
12/99	Rental list	2000	1	20

By doing a test you will find how your compiled list is doing versus your rental list and house list. Your house list will in most cases outpull all other lists. In the test above, the compiled list pulled as high a percentage as the costly rental list. Your chief goal will be to increase your sales to increase your most important list: your house list.

Some catalog marketers who spend the time and effort to compile a specialized list will rent it to others and gain additional revenue to compile additional lists or to use in their catalog business. Below you will find some compiled lists which are now rented to catalog marketers and mail order owners:

Consultants   Public accountants
Attorneys   Contractors
English teachers   Child care centers
Small publishers   Machine shops
Newsletter owners   Nursing homes
Libraries   Gift stores
Gourmet cooks

Compiled lists are expensive to build both in time and, since time is money, in money. The value of the compiled list is that you have complete ownership of it, and you can either sell or rent it out.

Make your product multidimensional

Make your product come alive in the eyes and ears of your readers by showing how it relates to a special event or an important cause in your business field, region, or country. For example, a marketer of baking supplies developed a catalog showing a special event—a "Bake the Largest Cake" contest—to add interest in the products and the catalog. Do whatever you can do to add interest in the complete reading of your catalog. Another catalog marketer stresses the full guarantee of all her products and how each product is selected based on being environmentally sound for the planet. This approach must be planned and continued issue after issue to educate your readers and customers to your total commitment. Avoid changing your approaches and issues; doing so will only confuse your readers, potential customers, and customers.

A catalog marketer of running clothing and equipment decided to follow a concept to increase interest in running and purchasing more running-related products by showing how running can be a group sport. To round out the concept, the catalog shows products and services to help other family members, including children and grandparents, join into the running sport. The new concept shows how all members of the runners' families can enjoy the various cities' and states' running events and marathons. The multidimensional approach can be further extended by donating a percentage of your total sales to a worthy charity which would be known to your customers or potential customers. Take the time and effort to test each approach to see which one will work for you and your business.

Review your marketing progress regularly

Successful catalog marketers set goals for themselves on a monthly, quarterly, and yearly basis. Once these goals are set, these marketers then measure their progress each month. Just like the rental store which compares its sales for the same day last year, the contemporary marketer is willing to focus on progress, and, when it falls below the mark, make the important decisions to get back on track. Once a New York catalog marketer of gifts found that she was below her sales forecast, and she evaluated how her competition was selling their products. After careful testing, she determined that more products in her catalog would make it a better selling piece, and now the sales are reaching and in some months exceeding her forecast. Forecasting is difficult at first, but it serves as an important direction setter to keep you and your business moving ahead.

Nothing lasts forever

Your catalog can be a huge success for one issue, but you cannot rely on this success; you must make the catalog even better for the next issue. Your copy approach might hit it just right for the fall issue of your catalog but fall flat in your spring issue. Your classified or small-space advertisement might bring you hundreds, even thousands, of inquiries for issue after issue, month after month, but eventually the ad will get stale, and the action will begin to slow and finally stop. You might change the advertisement to start the new series of responses to your catalog offers. For example, one catalog owner stressed new benefits in her catalog, another owner showed how much money could be earned using the products, and the responses increased. Good marketing management never stands still but makes the necessary decisions to keep the business going strong.

You are the president of your business

Successful businesses never just happen. Since uncertainty and change are commonplace, you need to take control by assessing information to serve your customers even better than your competition. You cannot just react to the needs of your customers, your market, or the business condition. You need information in order to make the necessary marketing decisions.

Information is essential to survive, grow, and prosper in your catalog marketing business. This information is marketing research and can be used for both the large and small business. Marketing research is the gathering, recording, and analyzing of data on the transfer of sale from your product or service from your catalog to your consumer. Such research can be as informal as simply asking your customers or potential customers what new products or services they would buy from you or as formal as a very complicated analysis or report on what customers are buying from your catalog in a six-month to one-year period.

With this important information you can then add value to your catalog by offering your consumers your best sales or marketing offer. For example, one catalog marketer decided to give a 10 percent discount on products purchased for a birthday present. Birthdays are important to your catalog potential sales, and you should also consider doing something special for Mother's Day, Father's Day, anniversaries, graduations, or shower gifts.

Another catalog marketer in Wyoming determined by a simple questionnaire that her customers wanted better prices for a grouping of products. After reviewing her products Jill decided to group three related products for a special price of $59.95, and the sales began to increase immediately. For example, certain related gift products can be brought together as a group, or three books on subjects such as starting a business, records for a small business, and marketing for the small business can be sold as a group. Review your catalog not as the owner of the business but as a potential customer and see which products and services your can group for the maximum sales and profit advantage.

Pat Sedler, owner of an antique business in Massachusetts, did some marketing research and found that many of her customers wanted the opportunity to review her products at home rather than make a decision at the antique shop or at the antique show. Pat decided to put together a small catalog featuring her antique jewelry, clothing, and furniture. This catalog gave her business an opportunity to present the latest products with current, former, and potential customers. Many businesses can increase sales by presenting their products in catalog form to their target market.

Bill Harian from Ohio sells carpeting and related products to customers in the Ohio area, and his marketing research showed people wanted to see sample products before they were willing to buy. Bill offered free samples of carpeting, and, once potential customers requested the sample, he requested telephone numbers. Bill called the customers after the samples were mailed, and his sales are increasing very well. Follow up to close your sales.

Summary

Selling is everything. Find ways to get to your target market. Use the two-step marketing method. Use classified advertisements. Develop your own budget. Spend money for your marketing. Use directory listings. Start a directory yourself. Advertise in the best possible magazines. Sell geographically and segment your market. Get potential customers ready for your catalog. Send a free report, then include your catalog. Power marketing is essential in the twentieth century. Use power testimonials of your employees. Know the value of your customers. Solve problems. You are a salesperson—develop relationships. Create ideas. Use brainstorming techniques. Develop a sense of urgency. Marketing is selling what your customers will buy. Run catalog house parties. Sell your products at the office. Swap your list with others. Test your lists regularly to determine their performance. Compile your own list. View your products as multidimensional. Review your marketing progress. Keep up with the changes in marketing and promotion. You are in charge of using information to make the necessary changes.

17

Managing your business

Managing your business means following through with all things necessary to start and operate your catalog business. Management means setting up strategies to meet your target market and continuing to work to reach those strategies until you reach a successful conclusion. Management means using your most valuable resource, time, wisely. Good management means you care about your customers, and you put into place customer relations programs which place the customer first in your business. To put the customer first means selecting products and services which are the best people can buy, and it means doing all the things you stated you would do in your catalog. For example, when you stated you would ship your products within 48 hours and you guaranteed your products and services, you should meet your commitment to your customer. I like the quote from a veteran catalog owner who, when asked how he managed his business, replied, "I print, mail, sell, and ship and always look for new products to sell." The response is a good one, but it is not completely adequate, because in this business, like all businesses, the customer's tastes are always changing, and your job will be finding out what the customer wants and then delivering it in a timely fashion. You're in charge of doing what is necessary to help your business earn a profit.

Management means planning

Smart management means you step back after reading and reviewing all the necessary information about the catalog business and then do the necessary things to make it a successful, profitable catalog marketing business. One catalog owner from Tennessee claims her role, as the owner, is "to work hard to get anything the company needs to make the company succeed." If the company needs new products, she gets them; if it needs new ideas, the finds them. Proper planning is to get what the company needs in the beginning of the business, rather than to try to attain it later when the process has started. Good planning means seeing the end in the beginning of the process. Successful planning means seeing in your mind's eye your attractive catalog being shipped to a preselected target market, receiving orders from happy customers, and making whatever adjustments are necessary to meet your success.

Planning means doing an evaluation in the beginning to determine what type of catalog is necessary to make your business successful. For example, ask yourself the following questions:

	Yes	No
Do I select the best possible product or service?		
Do I know my target market?		
Do I have an understanding of my strategy to reach them?		
Do I specialize in my strong areas?		
Do I price my product or service correctly?		
Have I written, designed, and printed the catalog properly?		
Are my marketing strategies, list selections, and public relations sufficient to succeed?		
Do I manage my business to keep it growing and profitable?		

Proper planning means setting a sales figure or forecast of the amount of products or services you want to sell for the first six months or one year. The forecast gives you something to help set a direction for your business. Once you determine what sales you would like to receive for your business, then you would put into place the attractive catalog, the list rentals, mailings, and advertisements necessary to attain that goal. Remember, the sales forecast is what you expect to sell during that period. If you expect sales in the first year of $6000 per month, when you multiply this by 12 months, you will have a forecast of $72,000, for the first year of your business. You can also adjust the forecast up or down during the year as well.

Planning is looking at the objectives of your company and then using the resources and ideas necessary to make those objectives become reality. Planning means focusing on the important activities such as sufficient sales and sales promotion activities to succeed. Your plan is really a model, an idea, and you must work hard to achieve it.

Your profit and loss statement is essential

The most important information to see how your business is doing is the review of the profit and loss statement. This statement gives you the gross margin, which is the profit you earned for selling your product, without considering your other expenses to mail out your catalogs and ship your products. Your cost of goods sold will include your purchases from suppliers and freight costs.

The expenses include your marketing costs, which are the printing, rental of lists, and postage, mailing-related costs, and advertisements to get catalog sales. The fulfillment costs are the costs to fulfill the orders you received from your customers, including boxes, addressing, labels, and putting customers on the house list. General operations include telephone, fax, supplies, computer supplies, and other costs to run your office. Your operating income is what you have earned in your business for the year. If you have rented out your mailing list, this would be additional revenue and would be included in your total net profit. Table 17-1 is an operating statement for the Deluxe Catalog Company.

The key to success in the catalog business is to turn your back to the routine work and continue to plug numbers in your own operating statement for the first few years. How many dollars can you sell each month providing you mail out monthly to your best rental lists and house lists? Consider getting a return of 0.015 percent on rental lists up to 0.0175 percent, and your house list could be as high as 10 to 20 percent return. Get some quotes to print up your basic catalog, and estimate the cost to get it ready for printing. Estimate the cost of doing regular mailings to generate the sales you need to succeed.

Table 17-1. Operating Statement for Deluxe Catalog Company

	First year	Second year	Third year	Fourth year
Net sales	$100,000.00			
Cost of goods sold	40,000.00			
Gross profits	60,000.00			
Gross margin	60%			
Expenses				
Marketing	$35,000.00			
Fulfillment	5,000.00			
General operating	5,000.00			
Operating income	15,000.00			
Rental list income	10,000.00			
Net margin	$25,000.00			
Average order	$50.00			

Double your sales each year

I want to give you a challenge in your business. If you can get $100,000 in sales in your first year, and your products are high quality, your art copy sparkles, and you have excellent customer service, set a goal to double your sales the next year. If you can keep doubling your sales for five years, you will reach $1.6 million in revenue. You now have a business to grow with you, or an excellent business to sell to a larger company who wants to expand into the catalog business which you just built up. You might even sign a contract with them to stay on for a few years as a high-priced consultant.

1st year sales	100,000
2nd year sales	200,000
3rd year sales	400,000
4th year sales	800,000
5th year sales	1,600,000

Now remember, your first year you have start-up costs which you will not have in the future—you may even suffer a loss in the beginning, just as many retail stores take a certain time to target their market before they become profitable.

What counts is your cash flow

Business statistics show that the businesses which succeed are businesses with cash flow—they have enough cash to pay the bills, buy new products, mail new prospects the catalogs to increase the business, and reprint the catalog, or prepare a new one. Quality products are important to you because you will get fewer returns. Returns are troublesome because you might have to send a refund check to the customer, or the other option, the customer might decide to use the return as a credit on his or her account. A credit memorandum means you agree with the customer on the reason for the return and approve it. For example, say Sam Brown of Milwaukee purchased some sporting equipment from you for $100; a week later he returns $25 worth of equipment because it is the wrong piece of equipment, and you agree that his return is justified. You must enter his credit memorandum in your accounting records. You offer Sam Brown a refund, or tell him you will credit his account, which simply means you owe Sam Brown $25 worth of merchandise anytime he wants to purchase it. Many of your customers will take the credit and buy later on. This helps your cash flow because you can use the money to buy more merchandise, do your mailings, and increase your sales and profits.

A debit memorandum is used when you purchase merchandise on credit from a supplier and find the merchandise is the wrong color or size or is damaged, and you return the merchandise based on the terms of your purchase. When you return the merchandise you must issue a debit memorandum in your accounting records. This gives you the authority to reduce the liability for the merchandise you purchased. Now you are free to withhold payment for the merchandise, since you returned it. Notice how the debit and credit memoranda have an effect on your cash flow; they save you from spending money and they keep your accounting records up to date. These credit and debit memorandums will be entered into the general journal. Keeping up to date with these memorandums helps your customer service program.

Records are essential to manage your business

There are basically four records you need to keep a financial management grip on your business. These four records are the same for your business or any other business and include the sales of your product or services in your business, the purchases you make for products from suppliers and expenses to run your business, the cash received from customers, and the cash paid out for payments for your expenses. It is important to keep the payments made to suppliers current, so you can get future credit to make additional orders. Accurate records allow you to keep your eye on the cash flow at all times. To record these four basic entries, you can record in special journals: the sales in the sales journal, the purchases for your business in the purchases journal, the cash received into the cash receipts journal, and all cash payment into the cash payments journal. Remember, cash means currency and checks. Many accounting software packages are available to handle these four special journals, or you can hire an accountant to set the journals up for you. You could handle them in the beginning, and as your business grows, you can delegate it to another family member or hire it out to another employee. By doing it yourself, you get to know the accounts, you know how to determine your cash balance and whether you are making a profit, what suppliers are being paid, what returns are being made, and other essential information to run your business.

Know your deductions

There are certain expenses in your business which you can write off in your income statement. Expenses are costs associated with earning revenue. Every expense you use and record reduces the amount of taxes you will pay the federal or state government. Some catalog owners use a large file with various sections to it and then place the invoice and the check into it. For example, your postage expenses are a normal write-off, so when you spend $200 for a mailing, ask for a receipt and keep the canceled check along with it as proof of your expense. Below you will find some of the normal expenses for your business. Remember, as mentioned earlier in this chapter, to determine your cost of goods sold, add your inventory to your purchases, less purchase discounts and returns, and deduct your ending inventory. Here are the basic deductions for your business:

Advertising	Supplies
Bad debts	Taxes and licenses
Commissions and fees	Travel
Depreciation of office equipment	Meals
Insurance	Entertainment
Interest on loans	Utilities
Legal and professional services	Word processing services
	Art design for your catalog

Office expense   Postage

Renting or leasing of equip-   Printing expenses
ment, machinery, or auto

Repairs and maintenance

Some nondeductible expenses are personal travel and meals and utilities used for personal use.

When operating your business from your home, you must carefully determine whether each expense relates to your business and the generation of revenue for the business. If you're using one-tenth of your home for your business, show how your deductions for utilities, or electric or heating bills, reflect only the 10 percent of your total costs. Keep good records all year long, and avoid trying to put all the records together for the last year within a few weeks. Your accounting records are essential to your success; use them regularly.

Focus on a specialty area

Catalogs which succeed present products or services in a designated area to a specific target market. Instead of trying to sell everything, try to focus on a specialty area whereby you can give a more concentrated effort to your consumer. Do something you like. Do something you enjoy. Try not to simply please everyone. You must please yourself. When you try to be all things to everyone, you start to skate on thin ice, and you will fall into the water. A good example is the granddaddy of catalogs, the Sears catalog. Sears tried to sell just about every product from clothing to appliances to jewelry to houses. The company decided to terminate its catalog because it was not making the profits expected. One of the major reasons why the catalog division was terminated was the lack of specialty products; Sears failed to downsize its product list, and its target market became just catalog readers and not catalog buyers. Focus on your specialty area, and you can succeed.

Once you decide on your specialty, be persistent. Once a catalog owner from California started a catalog catering to brides, and, after two issues, decided to refocus the catalog into a gift catalog. Rather than take the chance of having to move from one topic to another, spend the necessary time to select the product line with which you feel comfortable, and then work your plan. In the catalog business you must build your house list so that the repeat customers are a large part of the total mailings for the year. By changing the catalog line, the buyers on your house list may not be interested in your new line, and you might lose them. There are many advantages to sticking with your line until you turn it into a winner.

Customer service is everything

The customer relations concept is something all catalog owners agree upon, but too often it becomes something written into the marketing plan, or customers are told how important they are in a letter by the president in the catalog. Customer relations is the process of prompt mailing, helping customers order correctly, solving their problems, handling returns, following up to make sure customers are satisfied with the products and services they purchased or were offered on a regular basis. A catalog marketing owner in Arkansas sends a personal letter to a national sample of the house list along with an evaluation form asking "How are we doing?" and requests answers on a number of customer relations and service questions. The questions relate to product performance, ability to get answers on products and services from the catalog company, ability to return products and services, or the prompt receipt of products upon shipment; space is available to all customers to include any other comments as well. This evaluation is given full consideration by the owner, and when a problem is discovered—for example, a number of customers are not getting anyone to help them return their damaged-in-shipping products—a process is implemented immediately to fix this important problem. Customers are very difficult to find, and every opportunity must be taken to keep them happy and buying. Stay close to your customers by using the evaluation form techniques, or simply write a letter to them periodically to let them know you care about them and if they have any problems, to let you know about them. Some catalog owners simply call a sample of customers every three months just to talk with them and see if everything is going all right.

Know the rights of customers

Customers are not the only thing, they are everything in your business. Without customers you cannot earn the money you need to run your business, pay for postage, reprint your catalogs, or purchase additional products. Below you will find a list of customer rights. Today's customers are difficult to please and very vocal and will complain to the authorities when they are not treated fairly. The most severe punishment you can receive will be when they stop buying from you and turn to your competition for their future purchases.

Customer Rights

Your customer has a right to a quality product or service.

Your customer has a right to return shoddy, defective merchandise.

* Your customer has the right to receive notification from you when you cannot ship a product within 30 days.

* Your customer, when the purchase was made by credit card, must get his or her account credited by the next statement date.

* Your customer must receive a refund check if requested within seven days after notification.

Your customer has the right to receive all your promises, such as return rights, guarantees, warranties, or free shipping.

Your customer has the right to have products shipped promptly.

Your customer has the right to be treated as a valuable part of your business, not as an unimportant obstacle.

The rights which have an asterisk next to them must be observed; these are stipulations issued by the Federal Trade Commission, and they will be acted upon when your customers make a complaint. Avoid the embarrassment and the potential fine by acting promptly on returns, and when you cannot ship a product, write a letter, send a postcard, or call to notify the customer of a situation. Then your customer can determine whether he or she will accept another product or wants an immediate refund check. Nothing upsets your customers more than when they hear nothing from you, and the product ordered from you is not in the mailbox. The problem gets larger when the check they sent you is cashed at their bank, and there is no product in sight. To avoid your customer notifying the local better business bureau, the postal service, and the Federal Trade Commission, act promptly and notify the customer of any delay in shipment or problem with their order.

Set up a system to handle requests for products never ordered. Most people are honest, or the credit system in our capitalistic society could never grow to the largest economy in the world. There are still some people who try to get products or services free by claiming they never received them and asking for a refund check. When you receive a request like this, simply check your sales records. When you determine that this individual never ordered any products from you, send a letter similar to the one given below to the person who sent you the letter. Keep a copy of it for your records, to monitor who is sending these requests.

Office Supply Catalog
986 Camel Rd.
Nashville, TN 00001

Order:

Dear Customer:

I was sorry to hear that you hadn't received your order. However, when your letter requesting a replacement order was processed, we could not find a record of your order, listed under your name, in our files.

Therefore, I regret that I must receive a photocopy of your cancelled check—please send both sides. If you paid by credit card, please send a copy of the statement of charges.

I am sorry for any inconvenience and assure you that with receipt of proof of purchase, your order will be mailed to you immediately.

Sincerely,

Allen Hindale
Customer Relations

Make some copies of this letter when you find that letters of this type of complaint arrive on a regular basis and mail them out immediately after you receive them. Another case similar to this one is when the order form is sent without the check. Notify the customer immediately.

Monitor your returns

Expect some returns; there are some people who buy by mail, just for the thrill of it, and, once they receive their goods, promptly send them back and request a refund. Sometimes mail order or catalog owners request orders and promptly return them for a refund, keeping the products just long enough to get the manufacturer's name or a closer inspection of your products.

After you take action on your return, take the time to complete a return file, it will help you determine what customers are returning and why certain products or services are returned. A return file is shown below; the source of the sale could be your house list mailing, a rental list, or an advertisement in a magazine:

Return Products File

Date of return	Date of sale	Source of order	Product no.	Value of return	Reason for return
1/2/99	12/23/98	House list	101-43	$39.95	Wrong size

Returns are costly; you must restock the product or send it back to the original supplier, which means extra postage and handling costs, plus you lose credibility with your new or established customers. Customers talk to their friends, and when they have problems they will tell others. Try to avoid this negative publicity by keeping your returns down to a minimum. When you find the same products appearing on your return file regularly, investigate the reason for it, contact the suppliers to see whether they can explain the returns; especially in the case of defective products, many suppliers try hard to keep catalog owners happy. Review the source of the order, which means it could be the new rental list you ordered or it could be the advertisement in the trade magazine. Perhaps the advertisement oversold the product, and, once the customer looked at the product, she or he could not justify the cost versus the value. A return file is an important record to see how your customers view your products or services, and it can be a yardstick to measure how you're doing in your business.

Get your catalog to valuable prospects

Top sales people win awards because they reach sales records within their organizations, and one way to do this is to get leads from other customers. Leads are people and organizations which will review your catalog and order from it. One way to get these leads from your present customers on your house list is to simply ask them to give you their names, and you will send them a free catalog. In Fig. 17-1 you will find a lead sheet you can use in your next mailing to your house list to get additional prospects.

FREE CATALOGS

for your friends and associates

Do you have friends or business associates who would be interested in receiving our fall catalog?

If so, we'll be glad to send them without any obligation on your part or on theirs.

We'll send this catalog with your compliments.

Or, if you prefer, we'll send them without any mention of your name.

Just use the space below to give us the information we need and return the form as soon as possible in the free envelope enclosed.
 Be sure to include zip numbers, since we cannot mail without them.

your name: _____
□ you may use my name □ please do not mention my name

name	please print
company	
address	
city, state	zip #

name	please print
company	
address	
city, state	zip #

name	please print
company	
address	
city, state	zip #

name	please print
company	
address	
city, state	zip #

name	please print
company	
address	
city, state	zip #

name	please print
company	
address	
city, state	zip #

name	please print
company	
address	
city, state	zip #

name	please print
company	
address	
city, state	zip #

Figure 17-1. Free catalogs for friends. You need continual sales leads to keep selling in the catalog marketing business, and offering free catalogs to the friends and associates of your customers will help you increase your sales. Many customers like to tell their friends about new products and services.

176

Friends have many common interests; when Mr. Lewis from Seattle, Washington, buys sporting goods from you, there is a good chance he has friends, associates, and family members who might also buy from you. This is an excellent way to get free, top-quality names; keying their names will help you to determine which names are working for you.

Watch excessive demands on fully guaranteed terms

Most people are honest, and pay their bills, and, when they issue checks, they have enough cash in their checking accounts for the checks to clear. But there are some customers who will try to return goods which were cared for poorly, after the normal guarantee has expired. I'm talking about the person who uses the product for many weeks, months, and sometimes years, and tries to get a refund or full credit. You are not obligated to issue credits in full to people trying to take advantage of you. I recommend that you review the customer's buying record and determine whether the volume of her or his business warrants this full credit. Excessive credits can hurt your cash flow and your ability to run your business. One catalog marketing owner found that excessive returns were being made by a business opportunity rental list, and the owner made a decision to stop the mailings to this group. The rule of thumb is to be fair with guarantees but set a limit and stick with it. As the owner, you make the final decision.

Manage inventory level carefully

Having inventory on hand saves you time and money because you can mail to the customer right away and hope for bounce-back orders when you include your new catalog. When you run out of inventory you must get your order to the supplier quickly, and, if you cannot ship it 30 days after the receipt of the order, you are required to notify the customer. Everyone in the catalog marketing business runs out of inventory occasionally, but when it happens too often, it will not put you into the best light in the eyes of your customers or your suppliers. By finding good drop shippers, you can avoid excessive money in merchandise. Try to get more than one supplier for each product you offer. Set a reorder point for each product, and make the order immediately. You might want to use an inventory record similar to Fig. 17-2. When your sales

Inventory record for catalogs

Inventory record						
Item			Reorder point			
Product			Reorder quantity			
Vendors for this item						
Date	Carryover	Received	In stock	Usage	On order	Total

Figure 17-2. Inventory record. You cannot sell unless you have enough products on hand. Nothing damages your public relations more than late shipping, because you have to reorder a product from a supplier. Keep enough products available by using the inventory record and daily updating it.

come into your business for the first few mailings, make certain your inventory levels are brought back up again. You cannot sell products unless you have the inventory on hand.

Count the products you purchase

Just as your customer will count the products and services you ship to them and notify you when there is a mistake, you must also keep your supplier honest by counting all merchandise and supplies before you receive them into your business. Never, never pay a bill from a supplier unless you compare what quantity is billed to you with the amount you received and check the price on your purchase order. Check the freight at the same time—if you paid for the freight yourself, the supplier should not bill you too. Notify the supplier of any inconsistency immediately, in writ-

Receiving inspection report						
Received from	Carrier name _____ ☐ UPS ☐ Air Express ☐ Parcel Post ☐ Express Mail USPO ☐ Truck ☐ Rail ☐ Shipper's truck ☐ Other _____					
	☐ Prepaid ☐ Collect $ _____					
Our order number	Date shipped		Date received	Date inspected	Inspected by	
Quantity	Description of item		Number of cartons	Weight of each	Total weight	Condition of carton	Condition of items

Figure 17-3. Receiving report. Products get lost or damaged in transit. Keeping a record and fully inspecting all products purchased will save you many dollars. You will also gain a reputation of being concerned with the full operation of your business.

ing, and keep a copy of it. Suppliers will be much more careful when you keep them on their toes. To avoid missing a shipment, make certain the deliveries arrive at a time convenient to your supplier and you. In Fig. 17-3 you will find a receiving inspection report; it should be stapled to the invoice and purchase order before the payment is made. Check the addition and multiplication on the invoice, since even with computerized billing, mistakes do happen.

Manage your time

You receive only 24 golden hours each day. Do you find yourself running short of time? Would you get more done if you had more time? In the following paragraphs I will offer you some ideas about techniques to use to get more out of your most precious resource, *time.*

Review the process. Just because something is done a specific way does not mean it is the only way to do it. For example,

Alice Smith, a catalog owner, decided to do away with the cover sheets of all faxes going out of her office and saved time and money for her department. Review each process in your life. You might be able to shorten it, or even eliminate it completely.

Commuting time needs an assessment. How much time do you spend each day getting back and forth to work? Just 2 hours daily is 12 hours per week, or over 7 percent of your time. In yearly terms, if you work and commuted for 40 years, you would spend 2.8 years of it just commuting. Use that time to concentrate on what is important to do that day. Work on your catalog, read, or write, if you can avoid driving.

Focus on your top priorities, and set a goal for yourself. Too often, people waste their time by watching too much television, doing routine activities which fail to contribute to their top priorities. For example, Alice wants to start her own catalog on computers, so she sets her own forecast each month, forcing herself to use her time to reach her goals.

Put a value on your time. You have worked hard to develop a reputation at work, people respect you, and your boss asks your opinion on a regular basis. How much is your time worth? Don't let others steal your time and money by wasting your time. Charge others for your time.

Avoid the crowds, lines, and long waiting situations. Avoid the bank or the ATM at 5 o'clock on Friday evening. Wait until the superhighways are cleared before you start for work, or simply get up a half hour earlier to beat the traffic. When you set up an appointment with your dentist, ask the assistant what is the best time to arrive to avoid the waiting.

Don't give in to interruptions. What are your interruptions? People? Machines? Routine jobs? Try to isolate the source of your interruptions. When you start on an important priority, keep working on it until you finish it. A big priority might be getting your catalog out. Many home-based business owners find that since they own a home-based business anyone in the family or the neighborhood feels free to interrupt them in their business. Don't permit this philosophy of others to steal your valuable time and your life. Do a time log similar to Fig. 17-4, and carefully chart your day from 9 to 5 p.m. Where are you spending your time? How can you avoid the interruptions and get your important work completed? Are you getting your work done in the morning during your high-energy lead time? Do you get more interruptions during the afternoon when family members return

Illustration—Time Log

Date_____ Name_____

Time	Task	Priority Number	Comments on Effective Use of Time
9:00 - 9:15			
9:15 - 9:30			
9:30 - 9:45			
9:45 - 10:00			
10:00 - 10:15			
10:15 - 10:30			
10:30 - 10:45			
10:45 - 11:00			
11:00 - 11:15			
11:15 - 11:30			
11:30 - 11:45			
11:45 - 12:00			
12:00 - 12:15			
12:15 - 12:30			
12:30 - 12:45			
12:45 - 1:00			
1:00 - 1:15			
1:15 - 1:30			
1:30 - 1:45			
1:45 - 2:00			
2:00 - 2:15			
2:15 - 2:30			
2:30 - 2:45			
2:45 - 3:00			
3:00 - 3:15			
3:15 - 3:30			
3:30 - 3:45			
3:45 - 4:00			
4:00 - 4:15			
4:15 - 4:30			
4:30 - 4:45			
4:45 - 5:00			

General Review and Comments_____

_____

Grade _____

Figure 17-4. Time log. Your time is priceless. Making certain that things run smoothly means paying careful attention to your use of time. Cut down on your time-wasting situations and get your top priorities completed by regularly using this time log.

from work and school? Notice that the time log offers you an opportunity to give yourself a grade. Evaluate your time use and make each day count to the maximum by cutting out the interruptions so you can get the top-priority work done.

Set a plan for each day. Each day is precious to you. It is 24 golden hours, with 1440 minutes, and 88,400 seconds. You and you alone have the important responsibility of making a list of what needs to be done to start and operate your catalog marketing business. Many business owners find a "Things to Do" sheet which can be used daily to list their important assignments and jobs. Successful time managers accomplish many goals by simply starting them after listing them on their "Things to Do" list and each day working on them until they are complete. Make copies of your "Things to Do" list and use them in your daily activities.

Avoid procrastination by doing it today. Why spend valuable time and effort stalling on something, or giving stale, nonrational reasons why you cannot do something? The first step on the journey from the stranglehold of procrastination is simply to start the project or idea. Time is life. Time is the resource you can use to accomplish what you want in life. Manage your time wisely, and get the best return on investment possible.

Turn plain readers into buyers

Before you approve the copy and artwork prior to printing, decide whether they will motivate today's difficult-to-satisfy-and-sell consumers enough for them to take out their checkbooks or use their credit cards to make the purchase.

Do you show the main product in action? Do you motivate the customer with words, phrases, terms which will create the desire to buy? Are your terms of sales attractive enough to appeal to your target market? What terms and special incentives are being presented by your competition? What special guarantee, warranty, special discount, or special value are you offering to stand out from the crowd? Do you make it easy for your prospect to buy from you? Ask yourself, would you purchase a product from your catalog? Why or why not? Is the catalog easy to follow? Is it clear and simple enough? Do you use the "you" approach? If you could make it more convincing, what would you do? Now do it. Never print up a catalog unless you are convinced that you have the best possible catalog possible for your prospects. When you send out a catalog with only adequate copy and art, you can expect only adequate results.

Use reasonable credit and payment procedures

Allow customers to use their credit cards. Research shows that prospects and customers will use their credit cards and will spend more per order when this option is available. Open an account at your local bank, and, after an initial application, a decision will be made on your account. There is a charge by the bank to handle these credit card sales, but it speeds up your cash flow, and you don't have the problem with any bad checks.

How do you handle a bad check? Immediately call or write to the customer, and inform him or her of the situation; oftentimes a deposit can be made immediately, and the check can be cleared at your bank. Some catalog owners just redeposit the check with insufficient funds, and when it comes back the second time with insufficient funds, the customer is immediately contacted, and told about the situation. Sometimes a money order is required to pay for the order. Most customers are honest and pay with good checks; occasionally a bad check will appear, but not too often.

Should you issue credit? Many catalog owners selling to businesses ship to them on a bill-me arrangement, and then must invoice the customer, wait for the money, usually on a 30-day basis. This is fine for an established catalog business, but in the beginning of any business, cash flow is crucial, so I suggest you avoid the extension of credit beyond the N/10 period, which is a total of 10 days credit.

Once a credit customer fails to pay within the terms extended, contact him or her immediately and find out the reason for the delay. Hold up any new orders until the customer pays the overdue balance. Extending credit is an additional service but an expensive one for the owner with the possible delay in payment, invoicing costs, and possible collection costs. Many businesses and customers can easily pay for the merchandise when they order it or use their national bank credit cards.

Manage how you handle customer complaints and your mistakes

Customer service is essential in the catalog business; customers can take their business to another catalog company without leaving their home or place of business. When a customer or prospect takes the time to write you a letter or to call you on the telephone or to send you a fax, this is sufficient reason to answer the complaint. Successful catalog owners not only respond to the complaint but try hard to solve the problem as well. For example, when you get a number of complaints on a particular product, review the product fully and talk with the supplier. What is the nature of the complaint? Send a new product; the customer is always right. Delaying a response to the complaint upsets the customer and make matters worse for you. The customer may then write to the better business bureau or the postal authorities, and you want to avoid the negative public relations. Set up a complaint record similar to the one below:

Date	Name	Subject	Resolution	Comments
1/5	Sue Smith	Damaged products #402-113	Replaced the product free	Contacted the supplier

Review your complaint file periodically and look for trends in product complaints, service complaints, or delivery complaints. Review customer service principles with your employees or family members. Customer service is too important to be enforced by only the catalog marketing owner and not the employees and contracted service people, suppliers, and even the postal or delivery services.

Manage your mistakes. Your catalog marketing business will have a certain amount of mistakes, no matter how hard you try to avoid them. When you find a mistake, avoid blaming someone or something; focus on a method you could use to lessen the damage of the mistake. For example, immediately following the printing of her catalog one owner of a tool catalog found that the telephone number was printed incorrectly. The proofreader did not find the mistake before the catalog went to print. The catalog owner solved the problem in a creative manner, she had some sticker labels printed stating that the telephone number listed on the order card was incorrect and giving the correct number. The label was placed on the center of the cover page. There were more telephone orders on those mailings than any other catalog mailings in the history of the company. Simply take the mistake and turn it into an advantage for you.

Use the telephone for sales promotion

The telephone is one of the most useful selling tools today. Not only can you increase your sales by taking orders over the phone, but more and more catalog owners are responding to inquiries by phone. Let's move closer and pick up the conversation of a catalog owner who wants to recruit additional dealers to sell his business products.

> CATALOG OWNER: Hello, this is Rita Long of Business Strategies Catalog Company. Thank you for your letter requesting information on our dealership.
>
> PROSPECT: Oh, thanks for calling me back. I'd like to know more about your dealership. How does it work?
>
> CATALOG OWNER: The total fee is $99. It includes merchandise, 500 catalogs, and a free list of names to do your first mailing.
>
> PROSPECT: Is there any training?
>
> CATALOG OWNER: Yes, we provide a course book which includes all your training, and we will work with you until you are ready to work on your own.
>
> PROSPECT: Can you send me some written details on it?
>
> CATALOG OWNER: Yes, I will put an application, catalog, and a full packet on dealership in the mail today.
>
> PROSPECT: Thank you.
>
> CATALOG OWNER: I would like to call you again in about a week—is this a good time to call you?
>
> PROSPECT: Yes. Please do.

Notice what happened here. The telephone call opened up a solid foundation to build a strong, lasting relationship with the prospect. The basic question was answered, and the prospect became more relaxed, so he or she could further consider the purchasing decision. Use the telephone to develop a closer and better selling situation.

Consider calling customers who have stopped buying from you. Give them an opportunity to order directly from you on the phone and tell them about your new and exciting products. You might even find out why they have not ordered from you recently. Use the telephone to increase your orders.

Learn cost per thousand names

Keep records of the cost of mailing your catalog out to 1000 names so that you can compare one list with another. Review the test below:

Date	No. mailed	Rental list used	Cost	Cost per 1000
Sept.	20,000	ABC	$1400	$70
Sept.	20,000	AMX	1200	60

By learning the cost per 1000 you can then project the costs of sending out 50,000, 100,000, 200,000 names using the rental list. You can also determine the cost per mailing, cost per advertisements, and many other tests.

Summary

Good management means setting and sticking to the strategies you need to succeed. The key management skills will be to print, mail, sell, and ship. Planning is essential. Set a sales forecast for your first year. Do an evaluation of your business. Review the operation statement each month. Forecast your future operations for the next few years. Double your sales each year. Cash flow is crucial for success. Know what role a credit and debit memorandum play in your business. Use special journals to save time. Read over all of them, use all deductions, watch personal items. Focus on a specialty area and stay there. Know and value your customers' rights. Obey the Federal Trade Commission rules on catalog and mail order operations. Do not ship to a customer unless you have an order and payment or have agreed to credit terms. Monitor your returns carefully. Ask your customers for customer leads. Review requests for returns which violate reasonable treatment and use of your product. Manage your inventory level. Count all products you purchase before paying for them—use a receiving inspection report. Manage your time. Convince readers to become buyers for life. Offer your customers the convenience of using their credit cards. Monitor those bad checks. Offering credit can increase invoicing, payment delays, and collection costs. Keep a file on customer complaints. Your telephone helps increase your sales. Learn your cost per thousand names.

18

Summing up

Congratulations for reading this book until the end! Now is the time for a summing up of all the key points so that you can establish a solid foundation and get your catalog started successfully. Successful catalog owners develop the central idea for a subject area, select the target market, and then prepare, print, mail, and ship their specialty catalogs.

Now is the time to offer the success steps you will need to get the best start possible:

Why You Can Succeed in This Business

1. There is need for specialty catalogs today.
2. Quality catalogs are needed by your target market.
3. People need a one-stop shopping catalog for your specialty.
4. Products and services are sold by catalog.
5. Direct marketing is a multibillion-dollar business.
6. Your lead product opens the door to other opportunities.
7. There are many products and service opportunities in the 1990s.
8. The challenge is to keep your customers buying.
9. You have the best of both worlds: your own business and one that you operate right at home.

Setting Up Your Home-Based Catalog Business

10. Choose a room, den, area of your home or apartment in a quiet area.

11. Spend time in that area daily; start selecting products, suppliers, choosing suppliers, writing copy.

12. A telephone, solid desk, and chair with a good back support are essential.

13. Use that room for your business exclusively; this is required for tax purposes.

14. Keep your surroundings light and cheery with light-colored walls and proper lighting.

15. Set up your books properly. Hire an accountant.

16. Choose the best business organization, a sole owner, partnership, or corporation.

17. Review your insurance and legal coverage when you start your business.

18. Check with your town or city clerk to get the necessary license or permits necessary to operate your business.

19. Manage your time to get started successfully.

20. Talk with other business people to get fresh ideas.

21. Select the best stationery—first impressions count.

22. Discuss your objectives with family members.

Reasons That People Buy from Catalogs

23. Convenience is important to consumers today.

24. People buy because your product or service can help them.

25. High expectations, timing, and a belief in you cause people to buy.

26. The strong appeal, excitement, and good selling help create good reasons to buy from you.

27. People buy from you because they feel you know what they need.

28. Get to know the decision makers and ask for the sale.

Choosing the Best Products or Services and Your Target Market

29. Your product and service must match your target market.

30. Choose a product you know and feel you can sell well.

31. Try to make the product or deliver the service yourself.

32. Your sports, hobbies, and interests are potential product areas.

33. Search for products in catalogs, trade shows, and specialty stores.

34. Contact suppliers to deepen your product knowledge.

35. Your target market is those people most likely to buy; they have enough desire and money.

36. Demographics and lifestyles give you added information on your target market.

37. Develop a strategy to sell this market.

38. Heavy users are important to your success.

39. Match your product market and strategy.

Establishing Essential Strategies

40. Choose a pricing strategy which works for you.

41. The customer looks at value and price together.

42. Test to get the right price.

43. Know your total price by doing a cost analysis.

44. Your promotion strategy helps you to reach the right market.

45. Tie all your strategies together to capture your market.

Writing and Designing and Printing Your Catalog

46. Get to know everything about your product before doing your copy.

47. Use the product yourself if possible.

48. Know the reasons, facts, figures which will help sell the product.

49. Test the copy to see what works for you.

50. Use line drawings, photography, and even clip artwork.

51. People buy based on seeing the product in use.

52. Typography is an important art form.

53. Review the various formats and possible catalog sizes.

54. Choose a theme which works for your products or services.

55. Become a catalog junkie; see what is being produced today.

56. Write copy and choose artwork based on your offer.

57. The copy and artwork work together to sell for you.

58. Do a dummy catalog first, and test it, before printing.

59. Proofread carefully before printing.

60. Your cover can be two- or four-color to add quality image.

61. Choose a printer that can deliver the quality you need.

62. Schedule your printing work with sufficient time for quality work.

63. Try to get the best price possible by getting a few quotes.

64. Examine your printing job before you pay.

65. You have an image to keep up.

66. Print sufficient quantities for future mailings.

67. Sell some of your catalogs to your dealers.

Getting Customers and Keeping Them Buying

68. Rent a mailing list which reflects your target market.

69. Test mailing lists regularly.

70. Build your own house list.

71. There are many different selections, from income to size of purchase, in mailing lists.

72. List brokers save time and money.

73. Keep buying new, quality products.

74. Update your lists—they age quickly—and keep them secure.

75. Review your house list profile regularly.

76. Mail regularly to keep your customers interested.

77. Inquire about bulk rate to save money.

78. Test the results of charging versus giving your catalogs free to inquirees.

79. Send your latest catalog when shipping to a customer.

80. Use the personal approach in all your mailings.

81. Keep the weight of your catalog as low as possible.

Public Relations and Marketing

82. Public relations is free promotion for you.

83. Use the news release regularly.

84. Send news releases to your target market.

85. Start a customer newsletter.

86. Invest in business cards.

87. Run your own seminar or trade show.

88. Sell your products or services to clubs, associations, and schools.

89. Appear on cable television and radio shows.

90. Build a medium network for your business.

91. Watch your phone manners.

92. Call talk shows.

93. Handle all sales leads and inquiries quickly.

94. Customer service is essential to your success.

95. Never delay a customer's order without notifying the customer.

96. Set up a system to handle inquiries.

97. Run small-space advertisements to offer catalogs.

98. Sell products at house parties.

99. Sell products at speaking engagements.

100. Nothing happens until a sale is made.

101. Set realistic sale quotas for your business.

Managing Your Business Successfully

102. Test your products regularly; drop the losers.

103. Know and respect the rights of your customers.

104. Handle complaints and returns quickly.

105. Learn why people return products and resolve problems.

106. Keep testing essentials, such as products, lists, copy approach, offers, and average sales.

107. Keep good accounting records, such as sales, purchases, cash received, and cash paid out. Know your profits on each sale.

108. Once you find an offer which works, keep using it.

109. Challenge yourself to make your catalog business grow.

110. Double your sales during your first few years.

111. Everything must be right to make your catalog business work.

112. Print enough catalogs to mail all year long.

113. Keep advertising and promoting your business until it succeeds.

114. Treat everyone fairly: your customers, employees, suppliers, printers, dealers.

115. Take time to enjoy yourself.

116. *Good luck* in your catalog marketing business!

Appendix A

Commonly asked questions on catalog marketing

Q. I read the book but still find it difficult to put all the principles together, such as product selection, choosing lists, and choosing suppliers. Where do I start?

A. Good question. Many of my catalog and mail order seminar attendees feel the same way. I suggest you choose one product or service for a starter, and try to sell this product using small-space advertisements. Once you sell some products or services, you gain knowledge and confidence in yourself to add to your product list and prepare your way toward a full-fledged catalog.

Q. Is there any set procedure to start my own catalog? Perhaps a list would help me.

A. Good idea. Below you will find a list of things to do. I recommend you start with the first one, then check it off and date it. An example is given below. You must start on one item, finish it, and go on to the next one.

Finished	Thing to do	Date
√	Review numerous catalogs.	*Jan.*
	Choose a product or service.	
	Select your target market.	
	Establish marketing strategies.	
	Develop your marketing plan.	
	Prepare your catalog.	
	Print and mail your catalog.	
	Develop public relations.	
	Manage your business;	
	look at sales, expenses, and profits.	
	Build your house list.	
	Reevaluate the process.	

Q. What are the most important principles to follow to succeed in my own catalog marketing business?

A. Knowledge of your product, the ability to see on paper, to describe your product or service in a unique manner, to turn one-time customers into regular customers, to keep testing to get everything just right, and to manage your business well. I find successful people keep a good relationship with their customers.

Q. I heard that the catalog business requires a lot of money. I know I want to start a catalog, but how do I do it without losing too much money?

A. Good question; it needed to be asked. Set up a budget of what you want to spend for the first six months or one year. After the first year, evaluate your business and determine what improvements and changes are necessary to make the business grow. Many home-based catalog owners find the first or second years in the business are nonprofitable, but by increasing their house list, learning which products sell, learning how to merchandise by catalog, and marketing for growth and profits they increase their business over the years.

Start small by preparing and printing catalogs which have a professional look, but avoid the four-color printing and expensive preparation costs until you can afford them. Present your products in the best possible way to sell them successfully to a clearly defined target market.

Q. What about sales taxes? As the catalog owner do I have to pay them? How does it work?

A. I was recently asked this question on a national television show. Yes, you are required to charge sales tax when you sell to customers in your home state, providing your state charges a sales tax, and repay the money to your state sales department. There is a possibility that catalog and mail order owners will be required to charge sales tax for shipments to every state, but a current law case will decide if sales tax should be charged for customers outside your home state. Contact your state sales tax department, and ask for an application for a sales tax number.

Q. What is the main association which deals with catalog owners and mail order owners?

A. The main association is the Direct Marketing Association, which offers membership, runs seminars, offers much information on the catalog field, and even follows up on business owners who fail to treat their customers fairly, such as by taking the orders and the money without sending the product or service. They can be reached at:

Direct Marketing Association
11 W. 42d St.
New York, NY 10036
212-768-7277

Q. I still need more time to determine what product or service I want to sell. Do you have any ideas?

A. I have included, as promised in the book, a list of products and services in Appendix B.

Catalog product and service ideas

Aircraft/aircraft accessories

Animal/pet supplies

Antiques/collectibles

Appliances

Arts/crafts

Art supplies

Audiocassettes/records/CDs

Automobile parts/accessories

Automobiles/antique cars/parts

Banking services

Bed/bath products

Bicycles and accessories

Boats

Boat accessories

Books/periodicals/directories

Brewing beer/winemaking

Building plans (storage buildings)

Business to business

Camping gear/supplies

Food/syrup

Furniture/home accessories

Gardening/lawn accessories

General merchandise

Gifts (wholesale/retail)

Golf products

Handicapped products

Hardware

Hobby supplies

Holiday items

Home energy saving products

Home/building repairs

Hunting/guns accessories

Industrial products

Interior decorating items

Jewelry, Native American

Jewelry supplies

Kitchen gadgets/supplies

Leather/metal craft items

Left-handed products

Canning supplies

Ceramics

Clocks/music boxes

Clothing/accessories

Clothing/children's products

Clothing/maternity

Clothing/lingerie/hosiery

Clothing for men/women

Clothing/formal wear

Clothing for mountain climbing

Coins/stamps

Collection services

Computers (used), supplies

Cosmetics (make your own)

Craft supplies/equipment

Crafts, general

Dolls (porcelain)

Drugs/vitamins/herbs

Education materials

Electronic games

Environmental products

Financial services

Fishing equipment

Flags

Flowers/plants/seeds/bulbs

Food, candy from New England

Food, cheese (Vermont)

Food, ethnic (Greek)

Food, fruit (exotic)

Food, gift baskets

Food, health

Food, jams/jellies (homemade)

Food, smoked ham and meats

Food, nuts

Food, organic

Food, N.E. seafood

Lighting (energy saving)

Military swords/collectibles

Miniature dollhouses

Motorcycles, accessories

Musical accessories

Musical instruments

Needlework supplies

Office supplies/equipment

Optical equipment, telescopes/binoculars

Pet books/videos

Photography supplies and accessories

Real estate (coastal properties)

Recreational vehicles, parts

Rubber stamps

Rugs (Oriental)

Science supplies

Shoes (hiking)

Software

Spices/herbs used for healing

Sporting goods/general

Stained glass

Stones/gems

Stadium seats

Stationery/cards/calendars

Stereo/radio equipment (used)

Tennis products

Theater/dance supplies

Tools (model building)

Toys/games

Travel

Truck/van parts and accessories

Videotapes/convert slides/movies

Woodworking

Yarns/fabrics/textiles

Appendix C

Twenty-six ideas to increase sales in your catalog business

1. Resell present customers.
2. Get better products and services.
3. Listen hard to your customers and inquiries.
4. Review other services you could sell and offer today.
5. Consider selling to government employees living overseas.
6. Schedule regular mailings.
7. Test your public relations and marketing regularly.
8. Offer a rebate when they buy over $100.
9. Increase your quality referrals.
10. Set up a telemarketing program to sell more.
11. Sell more and more often to your heavy users.
12. Consider sending out more news releases.
13. Get on a radio and television show to promote your catalog.
14. Get your catalog listed in free directories for regular leads.

15. Consider free delivery when a customer buys over $50.

16. Consider printing catalogs in Japanese, Spanish, even in braille.

17. Track the purchases by region; when western customers buy more of certain products, perhaps a special catalog or mini-catalog can be developed for them.

18. Develop new sales leads daily, and follow up with your offers.

19. Establish a strategy to sell to new buyers to replace the people who stop buying.

20. Run advertisements in target-market-oriented publications.

21. Resolve customer problems first, then resell the customer, not vice versa.

22. Tell success stories, show your customer how your products and services can work for them.

23. Consider using younger models in your catalog, so your customer can visualize youth and energy when using your products.

24. Consider showing minorities and handicapped consumers how they can use your product or service.

25. Position your products and services based on new demographics and lifestyles.

26. Keep up with the times.

Appendix D

Gallery of catalogs

The following are samples from several catalogs. Each catalog was developed carefully by choosing a product or service, a targeted specialty market, and a related strategy.

Catalogue Listings of
BUSINESS SEMINARS

*Fall
Seminars
Throughout
New England*

Nationwide Seminars   **800 642-4433**
"The Leader in Business Seminars"

Annual Update

Office
Supply
Catalog

Most Complete
Office Supply Store
Under One Roof

Office Furniture
Fax Machines
Computers
Office Supplies
Computer Books
Software
Maps
Mail Labels
Legal Forms
Copiers
Binding Machines
File Cabinets

Best

Small Business

Software

Computer Equipment Catalog

Disks
Cables
Software
Mouse
Modem
Paper
Etc.

END OF YEAR SALE

YOUR SPECIALTY CATALOG FOR

MODEL-T PARTS ▮

FASTEST GROWING HOBBY IN AMERICA

Restore Your Model-T To Its Original Condition

Hard to Find Parts
End Your Search In One Place
We Offer One Stop Shopping
In the Convenience of Your Home

**Model-T Parts Inc.
5 Park Plaza
Chicago, Illinois**

**Be the First in
Your Area to have
the Latest Films**

Your Full Catalog
of Video's

Film Fantasy

SPECIAL OFFER INSIDE

TOOLS Etc.
Spring Catalog

**Spring Clean-up
The latest tools available
for the handyman**

SPECIAL FEATURE:
  Helpful tips
  and shortcuts

PLUS:
  Discount Coupons
  Inside

TOOLS Etc., Washington, DC
(800) 243-8686

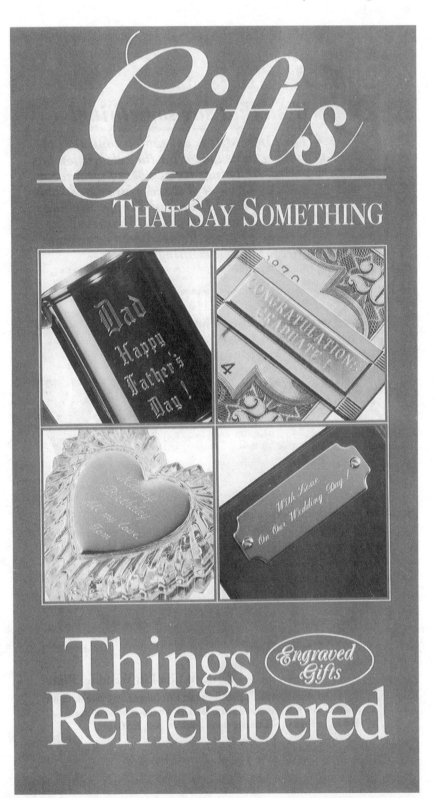

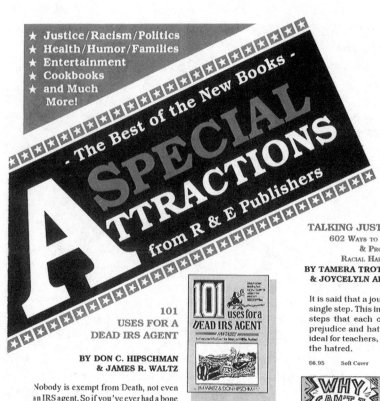

★ Justice/Racism/Politics
★ Health/Humor/Families
★ Entertainment
★ Cookbooks
★ and Much More!

- The Best of the New Books -

A SPECIAL ATTRACTIONS

from R & E Publishers

1993 Spring/ Summer Catalog

101 USES FOR A DEAD IRS AGENT

BY DON C. HIPSCHMAN & JAMES R. WALTZ

Nobody is exempt from Death, not even an IRS agent. So if you've ever had a bone to pick with the tax man, you're sure to love this book. The author has filled these witty and practical uses for the *corporate* remains of everyone's favorite dead person - the IRS agent. After reading this book, you'll be able to make your own *deductions* about how to get your revenge.

$7.95   Soft Cover   ISBN 0-88247-975-X   Order #975-X

CHRONIC FATIGUE SYNDROME
A RESOURCE GUIDE
HOW TO FIND FACTS AND GET HELP

BY PAMELA D. JACOBS

"Chronic Fatigue Syndrome can be an extremely devastating illness. People may have a difficult time dealing with complications of symptoms and treatment. This guide is an invaluable resource for accessing available programs and assistance within one's community. It can be a time and energy saver..."

Jeffrey Anderson, MD., *Corte Madera, CA*

This guide includes: CFS definition and symptoms, CFS Hotline numbers, self-help information, treatment recommendations, health resource centers, CFS organizations, and lots more!

$9.95   Soft Cover   ISBN 0-88247-951-2   Order #951-2

TALKING JUSTICE
602 WAYS TO BUILD & PROMOTE RACIAL HARMONY
BY TAMERA TROTTER & JOYCELYLN ALLEN

It is said that a journey of a thousand miles begins with a single step. This important new book is a map to the small steps that each of us can take on the path to ending prejudice and hatred. This simple yet profound guide is ideal for teachers, clergy and individuals who want to end the hatred.

$6.95   Soft Cover   ISBN 0-88247-982-2   Order #982-2

WHY CAN'T I EAT THAT?
HELPING KIDS OBEY MEDICAL DIETS
BY JOHN F. TAYLOR, PH.D. AND R. SHARON LATTA

It's hard enough to get children to eat healthy foods and avoid junk food, but when a child must stay on a restricted diet for medical reasons, that task can become monumental. This book will help parents to help their children adhere to life saving good regimens.

$11.95   Soft Cover   ISBN 0-88247-981-4   Order #981-4

WAITING FOR THE BANANA PEEL...
WE DID IT LIVE!
THE EARLY TV SHOWS OF DICK VAN DYKE & FRAN ADAMS
BY FRAN KEARTON

This delightful book has captured the energy and fun of those exciting early days of television. It is a nostalgic look at TV and America as they once were, but will never be again.

$22.95   Soft Cover   ISBN 0-88247-977-6   Order #977-6

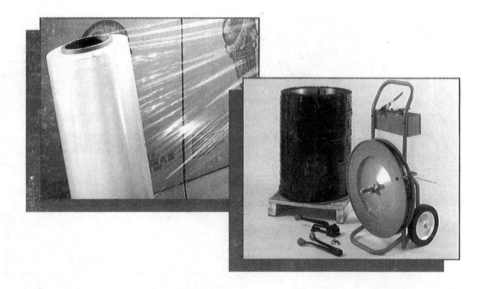

ULINE

SHIPPING SUPPLY SPECIALISTS

- ORDER BY 4 PM FOR SAME DAY SHIPPING

- ALL ITEMS IN STOCK FOR IMMEDIATE SHIPMENT

- QUALITY PRODUCTS AND SERVICE

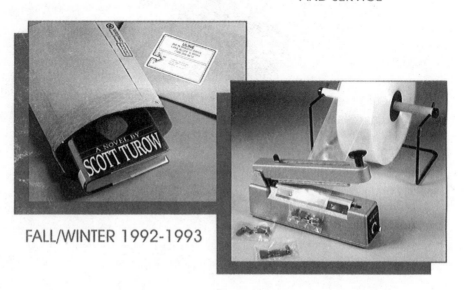

FALL/WINTER 1992-1993

MAKE ULINE YOUR LINE

Index

About the Author

William J. Bond is a writer, teacher, seminar leader, and entrepreneur. He is the author of *Home-Based Mail Order, Home-Based Newsletter Publishing, 1001 Ways to Beat the Time Trap,* and *199 Time Waster Situations.* A frequent contributor to magazines, he is also a popular speaker to business and service organizations nationwide.